DISCOVERING THE JOY OF
CATALYTIC
GIVING
FOR CHRIST

DISCOVERING THE JOY OF
CATALYTIC GIVING FOR CHRIST

JAMES P. GILLS, M.D.

Scripture quotations marked KJV are from the King James Version of the Bible.

Design Director: Justin Evans
Cover design by Justin Evans

Visit the author's website: www.stlukeseye.com

Library of Congress Cataloging-in-Publication Data: 2014956288
International Standard Book Number: 978-1-62998-407-0
E-book International Standard Book Number: 978-1-62998- 408-7

First edition

15 16 17 18 19 — 987654321
Printed in the United States of America

DEDICATION

To my friend and colleague,
Dois Rosser,

and to all servant–stewards of Christ like him
who invest their lives in the supreme joy of
catalytic giving to help others around the world
to receive the anointed Word of God, which
empowers them to grow into spiritual maturity
as sons and daughters of God.

———∞∞∞———

CONTENTS

⸺∞⸺

INTRODUCTION

———— ∞∞ ————

T HE REAL-LIFE STORIES written here are of godly men and women who have discovered the supreme joy of a lifestyle that focuses their divine abilities, spiritual giftings, and material resources on sharing the love of God with others. Their passion is to become mentors of precious people around the world in order to help them experience this divine love that has so transformed their own lives.

Christ's love has freed them from selfish personal endeavors and allowed them to pour their lives into sharing His love with others. Their chief motivation is the supreme joy they have discovered in catalytic giving for Him. To this end, they have chosen to:

※ Seek out the extremely needy—those in poverty-ridden nations making approximately one dollar a day—and to see these lives transformed, spiritually and physically, by introducing them to the teachings of Christ, His redemptive love, and hope-filled promises for abundant living.

※ Live personally on the least amount of their income possible in order to invest more into the lives of others and give them the opportunity to know the joy-filled life in Christ. Some, who are able, live on less than a tithe of their total income, investing the remainder of their income (after satisfying governmental taxation requirements) into sharing the gospel with others.

※ To live before the face of God (*coram Deo*) and be motivated by His divine love to pour out their lives effectively for others—not out of religious obligation, nor to keep the commandments; not out of the pride of receiving accolades from others.

These incredible testimonies are accounts of extraordinarily successful entrepreneurs, businessmen and women, Bible teachers, and other gifted servants of God who have dedicated themselves to:

⁕ Motivate others to the wisdom and joy of catalytic giving, which exponentially multiplies the effectiveness of divine giftings and abilities, efforts, and dollars to the end of spurring the Word of God to reach the souls of men and women around the globe.

⁕ Teach believers to seek out authentic, Christ-centered ministries and organizations whose track records show they are effectively leading people into personal redemption through Christ, mentoring them to learn to rest in His redemption and grow to Christian maturity through His grace and love.

⁕ And to encourage them to join their efforts with these effective ministries, which utilize the powerful principle of catalytic giving as a means of leveraging the generous giving of their donors, while minimizing overhead costs, for greater impact in reaching souls for Christ in the nations.

There is a dynamo of testimony within the pages of this small book that can ignite the same passion in believers' hearts—in your heart—that these extremely joyful servants of God are experiencing today. Their harvest fields can become yours; their joy-filled passion to reach souls for Christ can be yours as well.

No matter your previous disappointments from lackluster results of well-meaning efforts to share God's love with others, you can begin to enjoy the exponential rewards through catalytic giving that these servants of God are experiencing. Whether you are offering your expertise, your time, or your financial resources to reach the hearts of people with the love of God, you will see your harvest multiplied by thirty, sixty, or one hundred fold as you join with men and women who are motivated by the joy they have discovered in catalytic giving—for Him.

Man's chief end is to glorify God, and to enjoy him forever.

Westminster Short Catechism[1]

D EAR READER

In this chapter, you will be introduced to an exciting missions investment model that can multiply the harvest of each dollar you donate by three to six times now and one hundred times in twenty years. The results of this incredible missions giving model have been the phenomenal harvest of souls by International Cooperating Ministries (ICM) through ongoing church-building in sixty-nine countries to date.

Through matching and multiplying funds, ICM is faithfully stewarding all missions donations for greater returns.

How does this multiplication work? Over five thousand churches that have been built in these nations have themselves planted an additional thirty-two thousand churches. That means each of the churches that has been built has produced another 6.4 churches within the average of a decade.

It is gratifying for those of us who partner with ICM to know that every donation of two dollars they receive from United States donors is matched with one dollar. That makes one dollar and fifty cents available for each dollar donated to the project from U.S. donors, a 50 percent increase in the original donor's giving. There are no overhead costs to defray. Dois Rosser, the founder of ICM, established the Rosser Foundation, through which he personally covers all administrative and overhead costs. As a result, including the sweat equity— laborers who build the church in country—and the land donated by the indigenous recipients in each country, the original donation is increased to six dollars: a six-to-one multiplication.

Then, multiplying the six-to-one increase for one church by the 6.4 churches that will be planted in these countries by that original church over the next ten years, each donor realizes an eighteen-to-one match for every dollar they originally donated to church building in the nations. Assuming a 6.4-to-1 match per church in the next ten years (twenty years total) will result in a one hundred fifty-one–times increase for each original dollar given. (Please see charts for clarity in Appendix A.)

This marvelous investment model established by Dois Rosser's International Cooperating Ministries is catalytic giving at its best.

Through matching and multiplying, churches are built in remote places where the Word of God is given to the souls of men. These facilities double as schools, childcare ministries, and Christian centers for the communities.

I feel so blessed to be associated with ICM, where we can steward our giving to such a phenomenal multiplication that continues through future generations. May God bless you as you become acquainted with this unique missions organization in the following pages. My prayer is that you will be inspired to give to this church-building effort in the nations so that the anointed Word can reach the darkest places of the world.

Chapter 1

THE JOY OF CATALYTIC LIVING

Loving God and Others

———∞∞∞———

O
UR UNIVERSAL QUEST for significance, meaning, and fulfillment in life reveals mankind's innate desire to discover the
purpose for which we were born. This powerful motivating force is a
divine gift that is meant to lead us into relationship with our Creator–
Redeemer. He alone can empower us to discover the joy of fulfilling
our divine destiny.

According to the widely accepted Christian doctrine of the
Westminster Catechism (AD 1646), "man's chief end is to glorify God,
and to enjoy him forever."[1] This foundational Christian tenant is
based in the Scriptures, which teach us to walk in divine destiny. For
example, the apostle Paul wrote, "So, whether you eat or drink, or
whatever you do, do everything for the glory of God" (1 Cor. 10:3).
The sheer enjoyment of our relationship with God is the primary
motivation for living a godly life. That is what I call the joy of *catalytic living*.

Catalyst is a term used in chemistry to describe "a substance that
causes a chemical reaction to happen more quickly."[2] From that
strictly scientific usage we have derived the broader definition of *catalyst* as "an agent—person or event—that provokes or speeds significant
change or action in society."[3] As we embrace this divine purpose for
our lives—to bring glory to God and to enjoy intimate relationship
with Him—we will become His catalytic "agents for change" in the
world.

St. Augustine declared in AD 395: "Thou hast made us for thyself,
O Lord, and our heart is restless until it finds its rest in thee."[4] He
understood that the true source of mankind's happiness and ultimate
fulfillment lies in cultivating an intimate relationship with a loving
God. Experiencing the joy of that divine love becomes a catalyst to
provoke significant change for good in our personal lives. Then, God's

love expressed through our joy-filled lives can become a catalyst for reaping a harvest of souls for Christ.

Catalytic living, then, is living life to its fullest possible satisfaction and fulfillment, as God intended us to live. The real-life stories that follow are about people who have pursued this universal human quest for purpose and fulfillment in cultivating an intimate relationship with God. They have discovered the indescribable joy of loving God and the ultimate satisfaction of sharing His love for others.

SHARING THE JOY OF THE QUEST

My friend, Dois Rosser[5], to whom this book is dedicated, began his life as the third of five children in the foothills of Virginia's Blue Ridge Mountains. His home life was built around family and church life, as was the accepted lifestyle of good Baptists populating the area of the country known as the Bible Belt. In his youth, Dois developed a genuine relationship with God, receiving Christ as His Savior at the invitation of a gospel preacher in a little country church.

According to Dois, his father became his chief role model for relating to God and to people—all kinds of people. In all of his life dealings, he demonstrated his love for others, regardless of their status in life. A worker at Newport News shipbuilding yard, Dois's father made an adequate living for raising his family, and he adhered to the standard practice for Christians in giving a tithe to the church of everything he made for the Lord's work. This stable, Christian environment in which he was raised helped to form the core values of Dois's life and prepare him for the destiny God had ordained for him.

Upon graduating from high school, Dois embraced his dad's strong work ethic, gaining employment in the shipyard. He attended a business college at night as he worked hard to advance his position in the company. Then, when he purchased his first car, his life took a surprising turn that would impact his future in several ways.

His bright red Ford convertible caught the eye of a certain young lady, Shirley Sutton, the most popular cheerleader in his school. He had secretly admired her, but she had never given him a second look—until the red convertible. When he saw her interest in the car, Dois offered her a ride. And, as they say, the rest is history.

Not only did Dois win the heart of Shirley Sutton, but his love for that red car also influenced his decision later on to pursue a career in the car business. But we are ahead of the story. After serving in the air force as an auditor, Dois was employed a few more years in accounting and management positions.

Then, through divine providence, Dois embarked on a career change that would equip him for the ministry God had ordained for him. At the time, Dois was unaware of that divine purpose being formed in his life. He and a partner decided to become entrepreneurs in fields of insurance and real estate, selling both commercial and residential properties. As Christian businessmen, they enjoyed good success in their new venture.

On one occasion, they were asked to list an automobile dealership for sale. Dois, who felt a desire to go into the car business, took this opportunity to purchase the dealership himself. Largely as a result of his Christian integrity in business, which developed the trust of an ever-increasing clientele, over the ensuing years Dois built a virtual empire of car dealerships in his area.

Life was good, as Dois and his wife, Shirley, raised three daughters and enjoyed great success in the businesses he had acquired. They taught their children the same Christian values and work ethic they had been taught and had pursued throughout their lives. They also pursued increased involvement in their service for the Lord. As a prominent businessman in Virginia, God gave Dois divine favor in developing influential relationships with men and women on Capitol Hill, in the White House, and in diplomatic and business circles.

As a Christian businessman, Dois has served on the boards of several influential organizations, including First Virginia Bank of the Peninsula, Food for the Hungry, Hampton University, Overseas Council for Theological Education, and Prison Fellowship. He was appointed as an advisor to Lausanne Conference for World Evangelism and, in 1989, was elected by Religious Heritage of America as "Churchman of the Year." It became Dois's chief personal delight to share the gospel in as many ways as possible and be a positive influence in the Lord's work with all his many friends.

PERSONAL DISSATISFACTION

Eventually, the Rossers realized an accrual of material wealth far beyond what they had anticipated when they began their lives together. Though they tithed and gave generously to their church and other Christian ministries, there was a growing dissatisfaction in their hearts regarding their service for the Lord.

Through Dois's leadership involvement in the many worthy organizations mentioned, his trusted advice and counsel were sought out by business and political leaders on local, regional, and national levels. He had earned the confidence of his peers through his caring and giving ways, motivated by his Christian integrity and desire to serve others.

Yet, he wrestled with his deepening desire to do more for God with his personal resources, including his entrepreneurial giftings in leadership, his time and energy, as well as his increasing economic potential. He felt God had blessed him in order to equip him to promote the kingdom of God in greater ways. But how to do that?

Of course, God was quick to respond to His son's divine dissatisfaction—but in a different way than he expected. It was during this time of wrestling with these life issues that Dois learned about a men's weekly prayer breakfast held in a nearby town. Such was the impact of the gathering that it was being called "the Thursday morning happening" in the area.

CATALYTIC CONNECTIONS

A local pastor, Dick Woodward, was speaking to a group of three hundred and fifty men at a six-thirty-A.M. breakfast every week. That in itself was a highly unlikely event during that era. It seems that pastor Woodward's powerful Bible teaching, seen on TV, was impacting the women who watched it, and they began to send their husbands off to Pastor Woodward's Thursday morning prayer breakfasts.

So, when Dois heard about the breakfast, he decided to attend himself. After hearing one of Pastor Woodward's lectures, Dois was hooked. He had never heard the Scriptures explained so simply and profoundly as in Pastor Woodward's messages. He was especially impacted by the ideas that the joy of our salvation was based in cultivating personal relationship with Jesus—and nothing more—and that God wanted us to enjoy a love relationship with Him, deeply personal and completely satisfying.

As he listened to Dick's teaching, Dois began to understand that finding the satisfaction he was seeking was not about *working* more for God; *it was about discovering the joy of intimate relationship with his loving*

Lord. In cultivating that relationship with his heavenly Father, he would find the personal fulfillment for which he longed. Loving and being loved by God, who is love (1 John 4:8, 16), would lead to a more profound sense of purpose in loving and serving others.

Dois confessed that though he knew Christ as his Savior and had read the Bible for years, he had never heard the precious truths of Scripture taught so plainly and practically as in Pastor Woodward's messages. He introduced himself to Dick, which was the beginning of a lifelong friendship and a providential partnership between the Woodward and Rosser families.

At the time, they could not have dreamed what the ultimate impact this divinely ordained friendship connection would have on their lives and ministries. Neither could they have imagined the phenomenal outreach to the nations of the world this catalytic networking of their lives and ministry giftings would produce. Theirs is a testimony to the limitless potential of joy-filled, catalytic giving. As a result of loving God intimately and desiring to serve others passionately, they would utilize their personal giftings, together with others, to bring glory to God in the decades that followed.

THE LIMITLESS POTENTIAL OF CATALYTIC GIVING

As Dick and Dois shared their like-minded goals to impact as many people as possible with the good news of the gospel, their giftings and resources would become a catalyst to impact nations with the message of salvation. As you read their story, I believe you will be inspired to allow God to leverage your "five loaves and two fishes" to feed the multitudes, as the little boy did when he gave Jesus his insignificant lunch (Luke 9:16). Whether in monetary giving or giving your life energies, time, and expertise, it is in fulfilling God's divine purpose that you will discover ultimate fulfillment.

Catalytic giving results in exponential results when we network our lives with like-minded people who share our love for God and for others. Such catalytic connections in the body of Christ not only enrich our lives; they make our Christian service an exciting, extremely fulfilling adventure. These relationships create possibilities to do *together* what we could not begin to accomplish *alone* for the kingdom of God.

Life-Changing Invitation

Dois visited India to assess the impact of *Mini Bible College* and the follow-up. When he arrived there, he was stunned by the human misery he witnessed all around him. Overwhelmed with the need he saw everywhere, he wondered what good his small efforts could accomplish in that impoverished land filled with millions of beautiful Indian people. That was when God once again intervened to bring hope to his heart for sharing the gospel in India.

In Dois's words, "I got excited when my friend told me that you could build a church in an Indian village for as little as five thousand dollars."[6] As a successful business entrepreneur, Dois had practiced the corporate financial principle of leveraging funds for a greater return. He had built his thriving auto sales empire in Virginia by leveraging the return on financial resources as well as with personnel and other vital business components. Now, he would investigate the potential for increasing the harvest of souls in the desperately needy mission field of India using the same principle.

Dois examined the biblical principles of giving in the Scriptures that parallel catalytic giving. For example, when Jesus taught the parable of the sower, He showed that good soil would produce a better harvest: "The good soil represents those who hear and accept God's message and produce a huge harvest—thirty, sixty, or even a hundred times as much as had been planted" (Mark 4:20, NLT). Making sure to invest in "good soil" would secure a predictable harvest and require stewardship of the "seed sown." Stewardship of the seed would be vital in order not to waste this precious, life-giving resource.

Through the years, Dois had sometimes been disappointed with the lackluster results of missionary endeavors he had witnessed. Some mission organizations he knew devoted large quantities of donor money they received to support staff and cover administrative costs. He decided to take a different approach; he would use the financial principle of leveraging resources, which had made him so successful in the business world, in order to produce a phenomenal harvest of souls in the nations.

A New Beginning

As a result of his new vision for reaching India for Christ, Dois Rosser, at the age of sixty-five, founded an international ministry dedicated to spreading the gospel to the nations. He called it International Cooperating Ministries (ICM) to signify its basis in the principle of catalytic giving, which would leverage resources of manpower, funds, and multiple giftings in the body of Christ for greater harvest. (Please see Appendix D for ICM's statement of faith.)

Dois then established the Rosser Foundation, through which he would personally cover all administrative costs for ICM. In that way, he would leverage donor giving by freeing 100 percent of the donors' funds to be used in spreading the gospel through international radio and church-building projects. His personal funds, funneled through this foundation, have continued to the present to cover all administrative costs of offices and staff needed to manage the operational logistics of ICM.

Then Dois looked for like-minded, professional employees with giftings and abilities, along with the passion to carry out the vision of ICM for reaching the nations for Christ. To that end, he employs a dedicated team of thirty-nine people who work from the headquarters, housed in a simple cinderblock building—a former warehouse. Dois Rosser insists on holding his team to a high standard for maximum return on investment into their missions outreaches. In that same way, he faithfully stewards the precious "seed" of donors to be planted in good soil for maximum returns.

Catalytic Miracles

Dois, who was a board member of Trans World Radio, decided to introduce Dick Woodward's survey of the Bible curriculum, the *Mini Bible College,* through their international transmitter to the nations— in their own languages. His talented and dedicated ICM staff began to give oversight to the translation of Pastor Woodward's *Mini Bible College* into dozens of languages for that purpose. They developed a targeted media approach using CDs, Internet streaming, and other means to distribute Pastor Woodward's powerful survey of the Bible to the nations.

In the late 1960s Trans World Radio (TWR) realized that the Caribbean, and specifically the Dutch island of Bonaire, was the best strategic broadcasting location to reach Central and South America for Christ. God blessed TWR with friends in high places who allowed them to lease the use of the land for their station for one dollar per year.

Another of the catalytic miracles of God's provision allowed ICM to reach many other nations with the gospel message.

Using this catalytic approach to giving to missions through international radio broadcasting and church-building in the nations, the decades that followed would allow the partners with ICM to reap an exponential harvest through promoting the gospel of Christ in many nations.

CATALYTIC INVESTMENT MODEL

When Dois's friend explained that they could build an eight-hundred-square-foot church in rural India for as little as five thousand dollars, Dois saw an economical opportunity to spread the gospel in India, village by village, to reap a great harvest of souls.

To leverage the funds needed in building each church, he would not purchase property or hire construction crews. Instead, he would ask the indigenous congregations desiring a church building to provide the land as well as the "sweat equity" for the church to be built in their village.

The Christians of the Indian village would build their own church. It was a win-win situation. When built by the local believers, they have the satisfaction of taking ownership for their modern facility as a result of their hard work invested in it. The church building becomes the most impressive structure in their village. While it is dedicated to spreading the gospel of Jesus Christ, it can also serve the village as a school building, as well as a facility for many other community events. That was when Dois began excitedly to calculate greater returns for every dollar donated to these missions projects through leveraging every area of the proposed project.

Dois explained, "We discovered that when we took the church planting to the grassroots level, it developed a nurturing aspect. For example, in India, there are six hundred thousand villages that house over 650 million people. That's twice the population of the United States! We can't send enough missionaries to reach every person; we have to equip the national."[7]

Dois continued to share with friends and churches his vision of catalytic giving to multiply the spiritual harvest throughout the nations. In essence, he offered an average six-to-one return for every dollar donated to ICM's mission projects. He explained how he was investing personally through the Rosser Foundation to cover all administrative costs associated with these projects. (His personal investment through the Rosser Foundation is the backbone of Dois's catalytic giving approach.) Without having to cover ICM's overhead expenses, the donors' dollars designated for specific projects are freed up to be invested 100 percent in those projects. Then, this Catalytic Investment Model begins to multiply missions' funds and efforts. Donors' dollars are leveraged for multiplication in several ways:

❋ First, ICM employs the principle of matching gift incentives through local donors. Multiple matches are often applied to the same dollar, automatically increasing it to as much as three dollars.

❋ Second, ICM only agrees to sponsor church constructions where the indigenous people can supply the land, which eliminates an estimated 20 to 25 percent of the construction cost.

❋ Third, ICM requires local congregations to provide the "sweat equity" (i.e., physical labor) for their project, which eliminates another 30 to 45 percent of construction costs to donors.

❋ Additionally, some indigenous churches are funded through joint partnerships between ICM and the congregations, or between congregations and local church-growth organizations. That means a thirty-thousand-dollar project could cost as little as fifteen thousand dollars.

❋ *Finally*, as part of the agreement to receive donor funds for their church building, indigenous congregations covenant to donate at least 10 percent of their income by giving monthly toward the construction of other churches in their country until the sum of their construction cost is met or exceeded. *That translates into 100 percent of donor funds recycled in due season for additional church-building projects.*

Catalytic Multiplication for the Kingdom

The following chart gives you a powerful view of this catalytic model for matching and multiplying your missions investment, resulting in the biblical thirty, sixty, and sometimes one hundredfold harvest for the kingdom.

Power of Matching and Multiplying				
Matching: "Finish the work, so that your eager willingness to do it may be matched by your completion of it, according to your means" (2 Cor. 8:11, NIV).				
				Cumulative Impact Becomes
	$1.00	Donation		$1.00
Matching Investment Today	50%	Matching Gift	$1.00 x 1.5 =	$1.50
	150%	Partnership In-Country Contribution	$1.50 x 2.5 =	$3.75
Multiplying: "Living in the fear of the Lord and encouraged by the Holy Spirit, it increased in numbers" (Acts 9:31, NIV).				
Multiplying Over Time	5 More	Daughter Congregation Multiplier	$3.75 x 6 =	$22.50
	Exponential	Next-Generation Growth	$22.50 x 6 =	$135.00

(For a similar table for missions in India with an immediate 6 for 1 match, please see Appendix A.)

A Superior Missions Investment Model

Robert Leatherwood, the development officer for ICM, explains the superiority of the catalytic investment model for missions over other less effective approaches to giving. He writes:

The catalytic giving model that ICM has established can help every sincere believer to make a good investment into the kingdom of God.

This catalytic investment model begs the question of which ministries are the best stewards of my missions gift. Which make the most efficient and most effective use of every dollar I donate for Kingdom purposes? We need to ask, "How is the money used?"

In short, how much money goes toward the ministry's administrative expenses, and how much actually does the work of the ministry? Unfortunately, some charities give only a small portion of every dollar donated to the actual purpose for which it was given. In contrast, with ICM's investment model, 100 percent of every designated dollar donated goes to the mission field.

CATALYTIC NETWORKING

Dois said that when he first witnessed the overwhelming need in that vast, poverty-ridden land of India, he felt paralyzed in his mind as to how one could begin to meet such need. As he prayed, he began to receive the idea of this comprehensive investment model through networking with the body of Christ. This vision freed him from the paralysis he experienced and filled him with excitement for reaching many precious souls in India and other nations of the world.

When Dois realized that, huge as India is, he could employ the catalytic investment model to change this nation, village by village, he was filled with hope and joy. He began to express his newfound passion for reaching India to his fellow Christians.

Dr. Emil Jebasingh, a Christian leader who became acquainted with Dois through a mutual friend, became excited as well about the possibility of building village churches in India. He connected Dois with one of his parishioners, a professional builder. After thoroughly discussing the possibilities, they decided to pursue their revolutionary vision for this catalytic networking of local donors and indigenous partners to build village churches in India. Today there are over one thousand four hundred churches in India alone with a plan to blanket India in six more years.

The first church built in India by ICM was dedicated in honor of Dois's father; the second as a memorial for his mother; another for his older brother. Here is the exciting account of the life-changing impact of one of these first churches built in India:

> In the village where we built one of the first churches, the Hindus had sneered at the Christians for years. "If your God is so great," they jeered, "why does He not even have a temple?" The Christians had explained that God's temple dwells in human hearts, but still, they yearned for a physical place to gather as a group and demonstrate that spiritual reality.
>
> The day we dedicated that village church, a tattered old man grabbed my arm. Through a translator he said to me, "I prayed for twenty years," his dark face split by a huge grin. "I prayed that a church would come to our village. It would take a miracle for that to happen. And now here it is!"[8]

ASTOUNDING RESULTS

To date, ICM has funded the construction of over five thousand churches in over sixty-seven countries and almost every region of the world: Africa, Asia, Latin America, and the former Soviet Union. Those five-thousand-plus churches have birthed over thirty-two thousand daughter congregations and equipped thousands of indigenous ministers to evangelize their own communities. ICM staff has also overseen the translation of Pastor Woodward's *Mini Bible College* into thirty-two languages, with several more in production. Distributed by radio, Internet, print media, solar-powered audio players, and cell phone apps, this Bible curriculum has the potential of reaching 4 billion people.

Incredibly, Dois's small staff continues to administrate this vast outreach expansion and is poised to oversee the translation of the *Mini Bible College* (MBC) into three new languages every year. Perhaps the most exciting inroads are being made in the distribution of MBC in the Arabic language, specifically in Egypt and throughout North

Africa. As a result, Muslims are responding to the claims of the gospel as they receive the truth of Christ in their own language.

Yet, this exponential multiplication of harvest fields reached is still generated out of the small building in Hampton, Virginia, with a staff of about thirty people. It is a true testament to what people of faith can achieve for God when they allow His Word to take root in their hearts and allow the fruit of that empowering work of the Spirit to fill them with godly purpose.

The ongoing results in regard to kingdom building have been astonishing as well in the indigenous communities. Villagers who lived in shacks with no running water or proper sewage disposal were inexorably drawn to these brick-and-concrete churches with steel roofs. The presence of such a building in their village represented something very real and powerful for their communities. Out of awe and curiosity, they visited the meetings held there and heard the gospel of Jesus Christ in their own language, many for the first time. It was a member of their own village testifying to the love and grace of Jesus Christ.

These wonderful missions successes were not without their challenges, even to the core of the ministers involved, whom God had providentially united to impact the nations with the gospel. In their personal trials, they would need to find the grace of God to fulfill the wonderful destiny God had opened to them. That, too, is a vital part of the real-life stories of people who discover the wonderful fulfillment of purpose through cultivating an intimate relationship with God.

Dois challenges believers to consider what they will have to show for the significance of their life when they die. What will you leave behind that testifies to a godly life of fruitfulness and impact for the kingdom purposes? Your life is given to you in Christ to redeem the time and leave a godly legacy as the work of the Spirit fills your heart with God's love for others. Wherever He leads you, your life will leave a mark that will allow others to follow God and know His love.

You [God] will make known to me the path of life; In Your presence is fullness of joy; In Your right hand there are pleasures forever.

—PSALM 16:11, NASB

The greatest joy is joy in God according to Psalm 16:11. Fullness of joy and eternal joy cannot be improved. And this joy is owing to the presence of God, not the accomplishments of man.

—JOHN PIPER[1]

Chapter 2

GRACE TRIUMPHS IN TRAGEDY

*And He said unto me, My grace is sufficient for thee: for my strength
is made perfect in weakness. Most gladly therefore will I rather
glory in my infirmities, that the power of Christ may rest upon me.*

— 2 CORINTHIANS 12:9, KJV

D URING THE DECADE following the beginning of Dois Rosser's and Pastor Dick Woodward's friendship, Dick began to
face a difficult physical challenge. He would need to receive the divine
grace promised in the Scriptures—"my strength is made perfect in
weakness" (2 Cor. 12:9)—to face this overwhelming challenge.

An active athlete, Dick continued to jog as he had always, when he
began to experience alarming physical symptoms. Severe pain in his
limbs finally sent him to the doctor and was ultimately diagnosed as
symptoms of a rare degenerative disease of the spinal cord. Its slow
onslaught would eventually result in Dick's quadriplegic paralysis, so
severe that he could not move a muscle. Yet, in spite of this apparent
life-altering tragedy, Dick's story is one of triumph as a result of the
grace of God he received to continue to submit himself and his life's
work to God.[2]

Throughout the intensifying ordeal, friends testified to this divine
grace that overflowed in Dick's life, as well as in the life of his wife,
Ginny, who cared for him lovingly, meeting his intense physical needs
on a moment-to-moment basis.

Though completely immobile, by the great grace of God working
in his life, Dick led a more active, fulfilled life during his last three
decades than most able-bodied people. The thousands of potential lis-
teners to his Bible teaching still have no idea that the man who gave
them biblical hope and explained so simply the profound truths of
God's love was unable to move a muscle. He was experiencing the
reality of trusting God through all of life's challenges.

15

The lyrics to one of my favorite songs declare Dick's testimony (and that of his loving wife) to God's amazing grade. "Through It All" reminds us that God gives us hope in the midst of our trials so that we might believe that He is using those circumstances to strengthen us and draw us closer to His heart.

Growing in Trusting Dependence

In his paralyzed state, Dick continued to write books and articles, meet the demand for personal mentoring and counsel, and enjoy his family life as beloved husband, father, and grandfather. Family friends said that Dick and Ginny's serenity in the face of this adversity was amazing. They overflowed with the fruit of God's Spirit: real love, peace, and joy. When asked how they could be filled with such joy, they would say it was because they had simply made themselves available to be filled by the Giver of such good gifts.[3]

In 2008, Woodward started a blog to share with the world the lessons of faith that had long since become the foundation of his ministry and the *Mini Bible College*. He referred to these lessons as *The Four Spiritual Secrets*. In 2010, he published a book by the same name. He has become well-known for his succinct statement of the secret of his victory in Christ:

> God has given me His ability in exchange for my disability. I'm not, but He is. I can't, but He can. I didn't, but He did. I don't want to, but He wants to—because I am in Him and He is in me.[4]

The Power of *CORAM DEO*

Woodward's moving life story has ministered to the hearts of many people in difficult circumstances, connecting the love of God to the pain of the hurting in a tender, tangible way. He had cultivated intimate relationship with God through a lifestyle of *coram Deo,* through which he was empowered not simply to endure his suffering but to triumph over it and bless countless lives.

Coram Deo is a Latin phrase that means, literally, "*before the face of God.*" It beautifully describes the divine empowerment of a believer who is learning to experience the intimate love of God. Through daily communion with Him in prayer and in the Scriptures, we develop a lifestyle of *coram Deo*. Scholars tell us this means to live one's entire life in the presence of God, under the authority of God, to the glory of God.

E. Stanley Jones beautifully articulates this humble, devotional relationship with God his inspiring statement:

> In the pure, strong hours of the morning, when the soul of the day is at its best, lean upon the windowsill of the Lord and look into His face, and get orders for the day. Then go out into the world with a sense of a Hand upon your shoulder and not a "chip."[5]

Because God *is* love (1 John 4:8, 16), there can be no greater satisfaction to the human heart than continually receiving His divine love into our hearts through the work of the Holy Spirit as we practice living before the face of God. It is as we learn to live daily in His presence that He teaches us and gives us grace, no matter how great the challenges, to fulfill the explicit command of Scripture: "Whether therefore ye eat, or drink, or whatsoever ye do, do all to the glory of God" (1 Cor. 10:31, KJV).

Though we were created for good works that emanate out of our deep love for God, we are not exempt from experiencing difficulties and challenges in fulfilling His purpose for our lives. In the ordinariness of everyday living, as well as in the great tragedies and trials of life we face—so keenly witnessed in our friend and colleague, Dick Woodward—we must never lose sight of the grand, divine scheme of things.

It remains a profound truth that we can face life's greatest difficulties with faith that our heavenly Father is guiding us and that His great love is sustaining us. He desires that we trust Him in such a way that we learn to rest in His redemption, living in childlike dependence upon Him.

A PORTRAIT OF HUMILITY

Perhaps the greatest hindrance to enjoying God in this intimate relationship of *coram Deo* is the universal struggle mankind wages with pride. The Scriptures tell us that through the pride of his countenance man "will not seek after God: God is not in all his thoughts" (Ps. 10:4, KJV). It is as we humble ourselves before God to receive His love and submit to His lordship that we will begin to enjoy His divine presence and receive His guidance for our lives.

John Piper, beloved pastor, author, and Bible scholar, lists the traits of humility that characterize a believer who has submitted his or her life to the lordship of Christ:

* ✳ Humility begins with a sense of subordination to God in Christ. Jesus said, "A disciple is not above his teacher, nor a slave above his master (Matthew 10:24).

* ✳ Humility does not feel it has a right to better treatment than Jesus got: "If they have called the head of the house Beelzebub, how much more will they malign the members of his household!" (Matthew 10:25). Therefore, humility does not return evil for evil; it is not life based on its perceived rights.

* ✳ Humility asserts truth, not to bolster ego with control or with triumphs in debate, but as service to Christ and love to the adversary: "Love rejoices in the truth" (1 Corinthians 13:6).

* ✳ Humility knows it is dependent on grace for all knowing and believing: "What do you have that you did not receive? And if you did receive it, why do you boast as if you had not receive it?" (1 Corinthians 4:7).

* ✳ Humility knows it is fallible, and so considers criticism and learns from it; but also knows that God has made provision for human conviction and that he calls us to persuade others: "A wise man is he who listens to counsel" (Proverbs 12:15). "Therefore, knowing the fear of the Lord, we persuade men" (2 Corinthians 5:11).

* ✳ Humility is to believe in the heart and confess with the lips that our life is like a vapor, and that God decides when we die, and that God governs all our accomplishments:

Come now, you who say, "Today or tomorrow we will go to such and such a city, and spend a year there and engage in business and make a profit." Yet you do not know what your life will be like tomorrow. You are just a vapor that appears for a little while and then vanishes away. Instead, you ought to say, "if the Lord wills, we will lie and also do this or that. But as it is, you boast in your arrogance; all such boasting is evil".

—James 4:13–16[6]

Learning to abide in Christ as Jesus taught (John 15) teaches us to wait in His presence to hear His voice as our good Shepherd. And when we humble ourselves to follow His will for our lives, we are empowered to experience His joy and satisfaction in fulfilling His purpose as faithful servants for our Lord.

Living in *coram Deo*, before the face of God, frees us from a mere sense of duty, obligation, or begrudging service for God. It fills us with joy and peace and the righteousness of Christ, which the Holy Spirit imparts to our hearts as we wait on God.

One Day at a Time

In an article called "Building the Kingdom: One Day at a Time," Jessica Burchfield quotes Dois Rosser as saying:

All of my life in the business world was preparation for what God has for me now. I am convinced that there are people everywhere that want to serve the Lord, no matter how old they are. But you know what? Just having the passion to serve the Lord, doesn't make a difference; you must put feet to your desire. Any person who contributes and tries to advance the Kingdom, whether serving soup at a soup kitchen or bringing a neighbor to a doctor's appointment, I think they are making a difference. We, as humans, look at the big things God is doing, but He's looking at our hearts. Build the Kingdom one day at a time through your daily grind. Just because you're in a secular business doesn't mean that you're not in the Kingdom business. Give, pray, go. Let God write your story.[7]

My Personal Connection

My personal involvement with ICM and Dois Rosser's mission began quite unexpectedly when my friend, Ted Venetidy, came by my medical office one day to tell me about his personal involvement in mission work. A single man, Ted impressed me when he explained the impact that some truly spiritual men were having on his life. He shared with me how delighted he was to be in relationship with these men, like Dois Rosser. He recounted his mission trips with ICM teams, during which he helped to build village churches.

When Ted mentioned Dois Rosser, who was from Virginia, the name piqued my interest. My grandmother's name was Rosser, and she was from Virginia as well. I decided to call Mr. Rosser and get acquainted. We discussed our family heritage on the phone and realized that we both were related to the same two French brothers that settled in Appomattox, Virginia, in the early 1700s.

There followed a personal visit with our families, which culminated in my becoming aware of the huge vision Dois Rosser had for building churches in the nations. I was especially impressed with the financial strategy of leveraging monies and involving nationals in grassroots ownership of their churches' construction. I have always tried to invest in effective missions efforts that could become self-sustaining, not depending on continued outside donations for their success.

Then I learned that my neighbor, Jack Eckerd, had already been quite involved in the Rossers' mission efforts. They first became connected as members of the board of Prison Fellowship. When Jack heard that Dois was building churches in India and that he had been part of the Trans World Radio outreach, he shared with Dois the love he had personally for reaching India with the gospel.

Jack was also impressed with the leveraging strategy that involved the people of India partnering together to furnish land and sweat equity to build churches in their villages with cash donations he would furnish. He decided to partner with him and made a big investment into the ministry. Before long, through divine connections with donors like these, hundreds of these village churches were scattered across India.

After my providential connection with both Dois and Jack, I began to encourage believers in our community to help with the vision of ICM to multiply the harvest of souls through matching funds to leverage their resources, as I had begun to do. Those friends who wanted to see the value of their missionary donations catalytically multiplied to meet the great need for establishing churches in the nations were delighted to partner with Dois's vision.

At the time I never dreamed I would have the joy of participating in the building of thousands of churches in India alone. I love giving to the ICM ministry because it feels like every dollar I give does the work of five or six dollars through the sound financial principle of catalytic giving (matching) for each mission project. As the churches match and multiply, each of my dollars donated becomes one hundred dollars of God's real estate in twenty years.

In short, this is catalytic living at its best. To use a biblical metaphor, it is the body of Christ functioning as God ordained it to function through excellent stewardship of our giving lifestyle.

Joyful Catalytic Living

Many times, our natural gifts and our spiritual gifts for serving others go hand in hand. For example, as an ophthalmologist, I am involved in medical missions to restore natural sight, with the added goal of offering the wonderful words of life to these patients regarding salvation through Christ.

I have experienced a deep joy and satisfaction in restoring *natural* sight to my patients. But I can honestly say that to give to people the gift of *spiritual* insight, which I have received through my personal relationship with Christ, is infinitely more gratifying. It brings me ultimate satisfaction and a sense of fulfillment of destiny for which I was born.

Through over six decades of life-journey into an ever-deepening relationship with God, He has led me into many venues where we utilize the power of catalytic philanthropy, tending not only to physical needs but to spiritual as well. Along the way, through divine guidance, I have networked with others in the body of Christ who share my passion for effectively reaching the nations not only with social and medical aid but through the power of the gospel as well.

Together we have pursued the principles of catalytic giving, experiencing the supernatural results of networking our giftings and abilities and financial resources to reap a wonderful harvest of souls. None of us, working separately, could have affected these results of establishing the kingdom of God in the nations.

Recently, when nominated by friends as a candidate for the Templeton Prize[8], I was deeply humbled to read their compilation of philanthropic efforts in which I have participated during the past six decades. Like snapshots of a family vacation help you to relive the entire happy event, this document showed me how the focus of my life, which has increasingly narrowed, is helping me fulfill my divine destiny. I have stated my purpose, simply, in the mission statement for my medical businesses and philanthropic efforts.

> To be a catalyst for Jesus Christ by giving the inspired
> Word of God to the souls of people and mentoring them
> to spiritual maturity.[9]

My friend and colleague, Pastor Gary Carter, articulates this mission statement in more personal terms:

> To daily possess for myself and then transfer to others the
> joy, awe, wonder, and satisfaction of knowing the Son of
> God in saving communion by the Word of God, prayer,
> and the loving service of others in dependence upon the
> Holy Spirit's power.

I do not consider the building of churches in the nations and the provision of training for nationals for medical purposes a mere Christian duty. Rather, it is the fulfillment of divine destiny that fills me with the greatest joy in serving my Lord and fulfilling the Great Commission:

> And [Jesus] said to them, "Go into all the world and
> preach the gospel to every creature."
> —MARK 16:15, NKJV

Of course, to be filled with personal desire to fulfill Jesus' command requires a work of the Spirit in our hearts. No plan of giving, however optimal or potentially rewarding, will appeal to a selfish person who is motivated by personal greed. I have learned that as I yield to the work of the Spirit in my heart through *coram Deo*, my desire for catalytic living is strengthened. It continually frees me from selfishness and allows me to experience greater depths of the love of God in my spiritual journey.

WASHED BY THE WORD

It is difficult to express the joy of catalytic giving that so fills our hearts with God's love and to share His desire to express His love through extravagant generosity to others. The Scriptures teach that "Christ also loved the church, and gave himself for it; That He might sanctify and cleanse it with the washing of water by the Word" (Eph. 5:25–26, KJV).

When you have been washed with the Word, you are changed internally in the way you think and feel, in your attitudes and desires. Waiting on God through reading of the Scriptures and in prayer, our minds are renewed to think the way God does about loving others. This is what happened to my friend Dois Rosser, who listened to Dick Woodward teach the Scriptures and realized there was much more to the Christian life than he had understood. The Word he heard filled him with new desire to know His Savior in a more intimate relationship. That new desire led to wonderful divine connections and resulted in amazing expansion of their serving others that is impacting the nations of the world.

When Dois heard Pastor Woodward's testimony of the encounter with God he had when he came to the end of himself as a weary pastor, husband, and father, he was moved to seek deeper encounters with God. In his desperation, Pastor Woodward had cried out to God, "I can't do this."

It was then that God reassured Pastor Woodward His presence was with him in this painful place of utter dependence on God's power. Submitting to God and learning to allow Him to live His life through us is a good place to be. It effects a cleansing of our souls and a pruning away of self-dependence; it prepares us for an entrance into a more powerful ministry and satisfying life in God than we can imagine.

Dois was filled with greater desire to know God as Pastor Woodward did. Yet, he never dreamed that God would fulfill that desire by leading him, at age sixty-five, to found International Cooperating Ministries. He could not have imagined that they would establish thousands of churches in scores of nations, with Dick Woodward's curriculum translated into dozens of languages. Dois describes his mission's work in these terms:

> We're not a missions group. We just come alongside Christians who are already working in their own countries, but lack resources. We partner with them—not in a parental or patronizing relationship, but as true partners.[10]

Why Buildings Matter

A theologically based article written by Brian Smith addresses the perception of some potential donors who do not see the value in what church facilities can mean in other cultural settings. Smith cites the Scriptures that teach the biblical injunction for Christians to meet together:

> Not forsaking the assembling of ourselves together, as the manner of some is.
>
> —Hebrews 10:25, kjv

This injunction to assemble together as the body of Christ necessitates adequate facilities to accommodate believers, and Smith cites biblical passages that reinforce the legitimate need for believers to gather in order to function corporately in their divine giftings as individual members of the body of Christ. He references passages, for example, that directly refer to the Christian community in terms of the analogy of a "building" or 'temple."[11] While Scripture does not explicitly teach the need for building physical buildings, the understanding of their practical function is clear in the analogy used for the body of Christ.

St. Augustine, in his dedication of a church building, showed his understanding that Christian mission and the "building" of persons in Christ can run parallel with the building of physical spaces that can support that mission. In his address he declared:

> God, therefore, will repay the faithful for acting so piously, joyfully, and devotedly by putting the faithful themselves into the fabric of his building, into which they hasten to fit as living stones (1 Peter 2:5), formed by faith, made

> solid by hope, and fitted together by love (1 Corinthians
> 13:13)...Therefore, just as this visible building has been
> made for us to gather in physically, so that building, which
> is ourselves, is being constructed as a spiritual dwelling
> place for God...Just as we are constructing this temple
> with earthly materials, so let us erect that one with the
> building blocks of virtuous lives.
> —AUGUSTINE (PATROLOGIA LATINA, 354–430 BC)[12]

The whole purpose for building churches is to get the anointed Word of God into the souls of men (the only two entities that are eternal). There simply is no greater joy in life than to see the light of God reach into dark souls with His Word and change their lives *forever*.

With this understanding that buildings do matter, leveraging the resources of indigenous congregations with local donors becomes an explosive means to realize those eternal realities. This catalytic power of matching funds to establish churches allows the body of Christ internationally to explode into joyous participation in the great end time harvest of bringing souls of all nations to Christ.

In essence, that is the reason God established the church, a body with many members, each with different giftings. Together we are equipped to reach the world with the gospel of Christ. As we determine to partner together, believers can truly be sent into the harvest fields as the Father sent Christ into the world, to bring the good news of His salvation to the uttermost parts of the earth.

This kind of catalytic living has the power to impact nations for Christ, as we have seen in these real-life stories. Walking in the fear of God, reverencing Him in true worship and intimacy of relationship fills our hearts with divine desire and purpose. As we humble ourselves to become dependent on the guidance of the Holy Spirit, He delights to show us the good works He has foreordained for us to walk in (Eph. 2:8–10). This spiritual reality has resulted in the harvest of thousands of souls through the building of churches in the nations.

The whole purpose for building churches is to get the anointed Word of God into the souls of men (the only two entities that are eternal).

Tribute to Our Friend and Colleague

As I have mentioned, Dick Woodward's intimate relationship with God, which he had cultivated throughout his life and shared with so many, caused him to triumph over his severe physical challenges. Through the work of the Spirit in his life, these challenges actually served to make him a more powerful and effective man of God.

It is with a deep sadness as well as a sense of great rejoicing I must write that during the preparation of this manuscript, Dick Woodward received the ultimate divine call for which he had lived his life—to hear His precious Lord say to him:

> Well done, thou good and faithful servant: thou hast been faithful over a few things, I will make thee ruler over many things: enter thou into the joy of thy Lord.
>
> Matthew 25:21

Dick Woodward entered into his eternal reward on March 8, 2014. Though we miss him greatly, we also rejoice with him as he continues to live—forever—in the presence of God. He is now experiencing the consummation of the wonderful eternal realities he knew in part while still here and which he taught to so many.

Dick's life example, along with his masterful teaching of the gospel, still carries great influence to generations who are following along to know the Lord. Indeed, the apostle Paul exhorted us to "be imitators of those who through faith and patience inherit the promises" (Heb. 6:12, NASB).

As a tribute to Dick's godly life and in honor of our friendship, I have dedicated the Epilogue of this book to him. It includes the eulogy given by his family, who are following in their beloved father's footsteps in serving their Lord. I believe their testimony of the godly example of this loving husband, father, and grandfather will inspire you to seek to know God and serve Him as faithfully, as Dick served Him.

God has given each of us the ability to do certain things well...If your gift is to encourage others, do it! If you have money, share it generously. If God has given you leadership ability, take the responsibility seriously.

—Romans 12:6, 8, nlt

Chapter 3

CATALYTIC ENTREPRENEURS

Made for a Mission

———— ∞∞∞ ————

RICK WARREN, IN his best-selling book *The Purpose Driven Life,* describes the spiritual dynamic that believers encounter as they seek to find their purpose in life. In his chapter titled "Made for a Mission," he writes:

> You were made for a mission. God is at work in the world, and he wants you to join him...God wants you to have both a ministry in the Body of Christ and a mission in the world. Your ministry is your service to *believers,* and your mission is your service to *unbelievers.*[1]

Warren cites the Scriptures to validate this claim of God on your life and His promise for fulfillment of meaningful purpose in the service of others. For example, Jesus prayed:

> In the same way that you gave me a mission in the world,
> I give them a mission in the world.
> —JOHN 17:18, THE MESSAGE

And the apostle Paul declared:

> The most important thing is that I complete my mission,
> the work that the Lord Jesus gave me.
> —ACTS 20:24, NVC

This divine revelation of God's extravagant love, demonstrated in the Father giving His Son, Jesus, for the salvation of mankind, has the power to change the selfishness of our pursuits. Encountering His love inevitably fills our hearts with desire to share His divine love with others. The apostle Paul describes this phenomenon:

> For the love of Christ compels us, because we judge thus: that if One died for all, then all died; and He died for all, that those who live should live no longer for themselves, but for Him who died for them and rose again.
> —2 CORINTHIANS 5:14–15, NKJV

Experiencing such love makes serving others the joy and fulfillment of our hearts. In the previous chapters I shared the stories of Dois Rosser and Dick Woodward, along with their teams, who, through their intimate relationship with a loving God, have been empowered to love others and fulfill their mission of reaching an amazing harvest of souls for Christ. They represent powerful Christian entrepreneurs whose leadership giftings are surrendered to God in such a way that the work of the Holy Spirit through them has impacted nations in sharing the gospel of Christ. We often refer to this strong leadership gifting as an *entrepreneurial spirit*. Men and women who possess this gifting are not content to work as employees; they are visionaries who see potential success for their goals in every kind of venue; wherever they see people and needs, they initiate opportunities for service to meet those needs. Christian entrepreneurs, desiring to please God in all they do, have historically amazed the world with exploits they accomplish for the kingdom of God.

For example, George Williams, the founder of the YMCA, and William Booth, founder of the Salvation Army, established Christian enterprises that have outlived them by centuries. The legacies they established through their entrepreneurial missions continue to impact the nations with their Christian principles and service to millions.

Christian entrepreneurs, exercising their leadership, organizational, and promotional skills in order to make their godly vision a reality, create catalytic results in their missions and service for God. However, their success requires that they masterfully—providentially—connect with and utilize the giftings and resources of other sincere believers who desire to create the synergism for a potentially unlimited harvest of souls for Christ.

DIVINE CONNECTIONS

My friend Willie Hunter is no exception to the impact the entrepreneurial spirit demonstrates in its endeavors when surrendered to Christ. Indeed, the potential for impacting the world with the message of the gospel seems limitless when empowered by the work of the Spirit through humble servants of God.

Willie is an anthropologist who, with his wife, Janice, has lived and worked in the Dominican Republic for almost half a century. They arrived in the DR shortly after he received his degree in philosophy from seminary with a firm conviction that they could improve the lives, spiritually and physically, of many beautiful Dominican people. From the time of their arrival, their missionary endeavors brought them very close to the extremely poor of this impoverished nation.

In these few paragraphs, I cannot begin to adequately detail the godly influence Willie and his wife have had, not just in the DR but internationally as well, in raising awareness and elevating the physical and spiritual standard of living for poverty-ridden nations, beginning with their nation of residence, the Dominican Republic.

For many years, I have traveled with my family to the Dominican Republic on mission trips to participate with other ophthalmologists in medical mission projects that Willie orchestrates in remote, rural areas of the Dominican Republic. In a single day, as a member of a team of physicians, we complete a thousand examinations, along with numerous eye surgeries. People line up for blocks to receive the medical treatment we offer, which would not be available to them otherwise. While we ophthalmologists do the surgeries, our families work in the clinics to facilitate the treatment of patients.

Memorable Beginnings

Willie describes my first mission trip to that nation somewhat humorously. We did not know at the time that our first meeting would create a lifelong friendship and partnership in reaching out to the Dominicans with the gospel through medical missions. In his words:

> A secretary from an eye doctor's office in Florida called to inform me that her boss, Dr. James Gills, was signing on to the Medical Group Missions eye project in Moca, Dominican Republic. She wanted me to understand that

because Dr. Gills routinely performed fifty-plus cataract procedures a day, I should be prepared to have an equally high volume of patients in Moca. I assured her there would be no shortage of patients. However, I wanted her to understand that the good doctor would be doing the surgeries in an operating room with a window covered by a screen to keep the flies out, no air-conditioning, a shaky operating table and a very small portable microscope, which had to be manually focused. And that he would need to bring his own cataract instruments.

On a Sunday night around midnight, Dr. Jim and his wife, Heather, arrived at our lodging in a Catholic Retreat camp near Moca, located high in the mountains. Dinner was prepared for them after their three-and-a-half-hour taxi ride from the Santo Domingo airport. Getting acquainted after their arrival, Jim crossed his left leg over his right knee, then untied and removed his running shoe to expose a white athletic sock red with blood.

Peeling the sock off the skinless foot, I looked at it oozing from about four feet away. I said nothing. Finally, I got up nerve to ask why his feet were raw. He explained that the day before the trip he had completed the Western States One Hundred, a little off-road, one-hundred-mile run over the California mountains ending in Auburn, California. I did not learn until later that his completion of that race catapulted him to national recognition as a runner and notable athlete.

After the bloody feet the night before, I think nothing will surprise me. I'm wrong. The next day at our 6:30 AM breakfast, I introduced the Gills to the other eighty volunteers. Several eye doctors among the group whispered in my ear the notoriety Dr. Gills had earned in their field of ophthalmology. They said he was the most experienced and respected cataract surgeon in the US and that patients had traveled from at least seventy-seven different countries to enjoy his expertise.

We loaded into vehicles to drive the fifteen miles to

the Moca hospital and begin our day treating a sea of patients. There were fifty-five patients scheduled for surgery, twenty assigned to another surgeon and thirty-five to Dr. Gills (for our operating conditions, twenty is way above average). We finished the day with the surgeries completed in time for us to be back up the mountain for our 6:30 PM dinner. I did not realize I was about to be surprised once more by Dr. Gills.

As we were loading into the vehicles for the fifteen mile trip "home," Jim told me he was going to run back. "Do you know the way back?" I asked. "Of course," he responded. He detailed the constant uphill route, correctly citing every turn. We passed him about a half mile up the road; He arrived a little late for dinner and assured me his feet were fine. I did not realize at the time that Jim was not only an avid runner but also a triathlon athlete. He was motivated by a passion to steward the health of his physical body in order to fulfill his spiritual mandate.

During surgery the next day, I told Jim he was the first surgeon I had met who could even think about doing fifty cataract surgeries per day (twelve thousand in a year). He quickly informed me that he had met Dr. Norval Christy, a missionary working in Pakistan, who was the real standard bearer. He was doing up to two hundred and fifty cataract procedures in a long day. In his typically humble manner, Dr. Gills responded, "I don't come up to Dr. Christy's knee."

Fascinating History

I asked Willie how these ophthalmic medical missions began. He related that when he arrived in the Dominican Republic, there were only ninety-two eye doctors serving five million people in the entire country. Surgery for the poor was practically non-existent; the wealthy had to travel to Miami or other cities in the United States for cataract surgeries.

In 1985, cataract surgery was done in a primitive fashion with loupes and intravascular procedures and without intraocular lenses. There were only two operating microscopes in the entire country.

Lasers, ultrasound, and retinal procedures were not available, and only a few optical shops in the largest cities offered eyeglasses.

Through the powerful concept of catalytic giving, involving sharing expertise to train physicians as well as increasing awareness and developing funding for medical missions, there are now over four hundred eye doctors serving the Dominican Republic using modern techniques and equipment.

I had learned that Willie Hunter and a colleague, John Shannon, organized the first eye projects using a beach house as their home base. After Hurricane David ravaged the island nation, the operating facilities were transferred to the Elias Santana Guest House. It was known as the "Chicken Hilton" because of its proximity to many chicken farms. The fascinating history of these medical missions by Shannon and Hunter is detailed in the beautiful book *The Million-Dollar Vacation* by Madonna Yates. She is the wife of Dr. Don Yates, extremely successful ophthalmologist and spiritual father to many of these early medical missions endeavors.

Willie's extraordinary entrepreneurial gifting, even without formal medical training, has made him comfortable in his role as organizer of medical teams and, ultimately, as medical assistant to the ophthalmic surgeries. His work required the many-faceted skills of an entrepreneurial spirit: master planner, builder, tour operator, ambassador, mediator, political attaché, world traveler, fundraiser, negotiator, and board president. His persistent pursuit of his mission would eventually lead to his becoming president of an international medical ministry.

Raising their three children in the Dominican Republic, the Hunters were delighted when their oldest, Nicole, decided to study nursing at Taylor University. After her training, she became administrator of the Elias Santana Hospital in their city. His wife, Janice, besides being the perfect wife, mother, and spiritual leader of their home, became the CEO of that hospital as well.

More Catalytic Connections

After returning home from the Dominican Republic, I attended a medical meeting of the International Eye Foundation (IEF), where I met Juan Batlle, a young resident from the Bascom Palmer Eye Institute. A native of the Dominican Republic, he was just completing his fellowship in retina-vitreous Surgery under Dr. Edward W D Norton, chairman of ophthalmology in the University of Miami. He had prepared a brief executive summary of his idea of a model eye clinic.

Juan presented his plan to Dr. Norton, who encouraged him to present it to the annual meeting I was attending. It was accepted by the IEF, and he presented it to the participants of that prestigious gathering. In the original plan, the eye clinic was to be staffed by twelve people; Juan would see financially disadvantaged patients in the morning and in the afternoon would dedicate his time to work in the private clinic.

As he presented his idea for this innovative model eye clinic in the Dominican Republic, Juan expressed his desire to help the poor, who currently had no recourse for treatment. He shared his ties to the DR and his background knowledge of ophthalmology in Santo Domingo through the work of his father, Dr. Oscar Batlle. Then he asked the attendees to help in any way possible for the development of such a clinic.

Afterward, I went to meet this talented young doctor with his dream of helping the poor in the Dominican Republic. After introducing myself, I asked Juan if he knew Willie Hunter. He said he did not. We continued to chat about his project and share information. Juan describes the import of our first meeting like this:

> When the meeting was adjourned after I shared my vision for the DR model clinic, the participants began to leave to attend to their numerous commitments. But one person stayed behind and approached me with an intense look in his eyes; I felt he was trying to read my intentions as he began giving me some quick recommendations about how to proceed with my project. That person was Dr. James P. Gills.
>
> He asked me if I knew Willie Hunter of the Dominican Republic. I answered quickly that I did not know him. Dr. Gills responded, "Interesting, because he has been helping the poor in your country for fifteen years." He added, "I will send you his phone and address as soon as I get home. You should call him. I will also send you a book written by Madonna Yates telling the story of your own country."

A few days later, I received the book *The Million-Dollar Vacation* by Madonna Yates. I read it the same night. Then I called Willie Hunter, as Dr. Gills had suggested. I was invited to visit a newly built hospital, Elias Santana Hospital, during the Christmas holidays of 1985. During my visit, we discussed our separate visions for giving the poor of this nation medical expertise they so desperately needed.

I shared with my wife, Yolanda, my exciting conversations with Willie Hunter. It seemed to us, after my thirteen years of medical training, that this connection was providential and the timing was perfect for us to join the staff at Elias Santana Hospital. I arrived with my wife and two children seven months later.

Before we were even unpacked, I went on my first medical missions trip, held in a rural location over three hours from the city. There, I performed my first cataract procedures, along with five other surgeons, one of whom was Dr. Don Yates, who was accompanied by his wife, Madonna. I was completely unprepared for a power failure during my first surgery. The delicate operation had to be completed using handheld flashlights to combat the darkness.

In spite of the primitive conditions, after this first outing I was hooked by the wonderful success of this medical mission with its massive delivery of eye care. Obviously highly respected by the local people, Willie Hunter had a special gift for organizing the endless lines of patients visiting the makeshift eye clinic daily. They stood for hours to await treatment in spite of the potentially deadly heat of the midday sun.

As they waited, other members of the team preached the gospel them. During our team's evening sessions together, we dedicated ourselves to prayer for the people and listened to beautiful testimonies of the healing work that had taken place throughout the day. I am still amazed at the volume of patients we helped through the synergism of everyone collaborating toward a common goal.

Since then, these rural mission trips have become a routine part of the residency training program at the Elias Santana Hospital. The experience of seeing thousands of poor people gathered around a school or athletic-facility-turned-operating-theater in the hope of having their vision restored, whether by receiving a simple pair of eyeglasses or through surgery, only enhances our joy in witnessing their gratitude for being able to see again.

I established a long-lasting friendship with Dr. Gills as a result of his passion for medical missions and the divine connection we experienced through that IEA conference where we first met. I remain eternally grateful and indebted to the Gills family for their generosity through catalytic giving to help make our operating facilities a success.

AMAZING PROGRESS FOR IMPROVED MEDICAL CARE

The growth in the quality and extent of medical care in the Dominican Republic as a result of the eye projects initiated by Willie and Janice Hunter four decades ago is simply amazing. The first hospital, Santana, began construction in 1984 and was seeing patients in 1985. Currently, there are approximately twenty-five self-supporting hospitals dedicated to ophthalmology and training programs for residents and others. Together they handle five hundred thousand patients annually and do fifteen thousand eye surgeries locally.

With the addition of the medical expertise of Juan Batlle and others, they began to train two residents per year. They now have twenty-four residents in training at a time and have graduated one hundred and twenty-five ophthalmologists, along with more than two hundred ophthalmic assistants, who came from all over the world to train there.

The Hunters have developed the three basic prerequisites for excellent ophthalmology training: a professional faculty dedicated to their students' training; a wonderful medical library, which was donated to the Elias Santana Hospital by Juan and his father, Dr. Oscar Batlle, with Dr. Paul Palmberg and others; and a great number of patients to learn from. (Of course, the Internet now offers rapid access to applicable medical publications as well.)

This residency program is unique in that they believe the training of the young ophthalmologist should not be purely a technical and educational experience, but also a moral, ethical, and spiritual experience. The honor code, the respect for patients' rights, and humane and passionate communication with patients, which requires dedicating sufficient time to listen and satisfy the patient's needs, are all part of their training.

In 1986, when their operating rooms were inaugurated, they had an immediate impact on the grave prevalence of blindness in the nation; indeed, these medical facilities became a national celebration for the poor people. For the first time, they had access to modern cataract surgery with intraocular lens implants, corneal transplants, retinal detachment surgery, and other ophthalmic procedures necessary to retain vision.

It took about ten years to complete the first hospital in the Dominican Republic; the second required another twenty years to complete. Currently, there are approximately twenty-five hospitals dedicated to ophthalmology and training programs for residents. They handle between eight and ten thousand patients a year and are functioning well, supporting themselves, and teaching others.

Redeemed entrepreneurship of dedicated servants of God created an amazing synergism for this incredible missions success story. While many entrepreneurs use their gifting for self-serving goals, they cannot imagine the fulfillment and satisfaction they miss from not giving back to those who need their leadership most. Only by allowing the Holy Spirit to open our eyes to the love of God for people in need can we live in the joy of fulfilling our divine destiny and the adventure of almost serendipitously experiencing God's divine connections with others.

As I have learned the power of catalytic giving, I have experienced such joy of seeing God's divine connections exponentially reap a harvest of souls in the nations. How satisfying to see the providential connection of bringing Willie Hunter, a gifted entrepreneur serving in the DR, together with another medical visionary in Juan Batlle, a native of that country, to facilitate their like-minded dream and help fulfill their divine destiny.

It is awesome to watch this redemptive work of the Spirit in hearts of men and women who love God and desire to share His love with others. Their catalytic giving has resulted in making an amazing difference, spiritually as well as physically, in the lives of many thousands of people on many levels. From the simplest eye care for an individual patient to the training of other professionals who will serve their own nations, the potential for greater impact through catalytic giving never ends.

Intense love does not measure; it just gives.

—MOTHER TERESA[1]

Chapter 4

JOY-FILLED ACCOUNTS OF
CATALYTIC GIVERS

—∞∞∞—

B Y NOW, YOU have an understanding of the powerful and effective model of joy-filled giving we are describing as *catalytic investment*. The potential impact of catalytic giving, involving networking with others, is so much greater than an individual's sincere attempts to serve independently in giving his time, talent and personal resources.

Catalytic networking with other like-minded believers who want to impact the world for Christ brings immeasurable returns that keep on giving. Motivated by the sheer joy of experiencing the synergy of working together to share the love of Christ, believers are truly fulfilling their God-given destinies. As I have mentioned, there are many ways to give and to utilize the principle of catalytic living

Every morning when I awaken, my eyes focus on a picture of Mother Teresa hanging on my wall. She is one of my heroes. Her endearing, worldwide fame emanates from her lifelong, selfless purpose to serve the poor and dying of Calcutta, India. As I gaze at her peaceful and joyous countenance, I read the caption below it of her words: "Unless a life is lived for others it is not worthwhile."[2]

As I have mentioned, to achieve that joy-filled lifestyle we must pursue *coram Deo*, living in intimate relationship with God. Through the work of the Spirit, He imparts His peace and His desire to fill us with love for Him and for others. Out of that place of intimate communion, we find our sense of purpose and begin to discover the joy of catalytic giving, of connecting with others to serve God exponentially with the gifts and abilities He has given us.

I asked my friend Robert Leatherwood, who was introduced earlier as the development officer for Dois Rosser's International Cooperating Ministries, to share some real-life stories of the myriad ways in which we can maximize our giving into the kingdom. You can know the extreme satisfaction of catalytic living in your personal sphere of influence and with your God-given personal resources. Perhaps you will see yourself in some of these stories that Robert shares and discover more ways to increase the effectiveness of your catalytic investment into the kingdom of God.

Divine Surprise: The Joy of Adoption

As the development officer for ICM, I have the unique joy of sharing the passion of many donors' stories and the joy they experience when God answers their prayers to be effective in bringing a harvest of souls to Christ. I am delighted to share with you a few of these real-life stories that illustrate the fulfillment of dreams that God gives to those who desire to serve Him.

First, I'd like to tell you the story of the Stanger family. As a professional investment advisor, Jim and his wife, Teri, conscientiously seek to invest in ministry work that furthers the kingdom of God and advances mankind for His good purposes.

Several years ago while traveling on business to China and hearing God's call of the Great Commission in Matthew 28:19–20 to "go...therefore, and teach all nations, baptizing them in the name of the Father, and of the Son, and of the Holy Ghost" (KJV). The Lord placed a desire on Jim and Teri's hearts to adopt a baby girl from China. Their family would never be the same. When you align your motives and desire with biblical principles, the earth trembles as God moves. He stretched out His hands and delivered a beautiful bundle of joy, little Theresa Maylei, into the arms of their family.

While waiting for almost two years for their daughter, God stirred upon their hearts to pray for her birth parents and others in her village in China. They prayed intentionally that they too would come to know the divine love and power of our risen Savior. God's sovereign hand was going before them. Providentially, a neighbor invited them to learn about International Cooperating Ministry. ICM was just beginning their vision to build churches in China. And as the director for Chinese missions in China, we discussed the possibility of their investing in the work of God in China by building a church. Specifically, they requested a church within the province in which their daughter was born. Geographically, this seemed initially impossible because of the dynamics and constraints of operating anywhere in China. But we agreed to try.

Several months later the Stangers' received a call from Dois letting them know that ICM identified a possible church location in China in a province that they had hoped was at least near their desired request. Little did they know that the church building would be located directly in the heart of Theresa Maylei's birth place and within miles of her orphanage. Once the building was completed the Stanger family traveled back to China to be part of the church dedication ceremonies. Located in a village plagued with flooding and poverty, the church is built upon a hill, a shining light visible from miles away. It is a refuge and a fortress where thousands can find shelter and relief, reminding them of the first-century church: feeding the hungry, clothing the naked, and providing rest to the weary. They witnessed the church fulfilling the Great Commission in the very village their precious daughter, Theresa Maylei, was born! They were able to witness the church teaching all nations and baptizing in the name of the Father, the Son, and the Holy Ghost.

CATALYTIC CHRISTMAS

Bob is a CPA with adult children. Each year at Christmastime, their extended families get together to exchange names and buy a gift for another member of the family. One Christmas, as the Christian leader of his family, Bob decided to give some re-direction to their Christmas giving tradition.

When his family assembled to draw names for Christmas, he asked them to bypass buying gifts for one another. Instead, he challenged them to take the money they would traditionally have spent for a brother or sister and invest it in building a church in the nations. The church their Christmas monies would build would become part of their family legacy, a spiritual investment with catalytic return for the kingdom of God.

Bob was delighted when his family caught the vision and joyfully gave generously to build a church as a Christmas gift to Jesus. I call it a *catalytic Christmas*, creatively giving so the whole family got involved and reaped a greater joy of giving than they could have done individually. Casting a vision for his family to see beyond the traditional ways of gift-giving, he empowered them to give a Christmas gift that would last for all eternity.

Catalytic Kids

I am so amazed at the many different ways our donors find to fulfill their passion for bringing souls to Christ. Sherry's story is one of the more remarkably creative ways to involve kids in reaping a harvest of souls.

You may ask, "So how can kids who have no personal income get involved in catalytic giving?" You have to give it up to Sherry, who loves and understands junior high students and their desire to really accomplish something meaningful with their faith. She says that kids don't want to sit on the sidelines; they want to get into the game.

Sherry is constantly finding ways for her students to serve others locally, so she had an idea that would help kids learn to serve people in a broader sphere—internationally. She challenged the kids to bring their weekly offering to class, whether pennies, nickels, dimes, or dollars. Teaching them the story of the woman Jesus commended for giving her two mites into the offering, which was all she had to live on, Sherry inspired them to find ways to give more each week to give to international missions.

Kids who often didn't have much at all to give began sacrificing their regular purchase of a Coca-Colas and candy bars at the convenience store, for example. They caught the vision of the woman who gave all. Sherry cast a vision for these kids that none of them could achieve individually.

Together they accepted the challenge of catalytic giving to invest in a missions project. As a result, there is a church in Tanzania today that was built through those kids' offerings. I call that extreme catalytic giving.

A CATALYTIC ANNIVERSARY GIFT?

I remember the day when I got a call from Dr. Pit Gills, ophthalmologist son of Dr. James Gills. He shared with me his desire to give a unique gift to his parents on their fiftieth wedding anniversary. Knowing his father and mother's supreme joy in giving to missions, Pit decided that he would honor them by presenting them with a special catalytic gift.

During their memorable celebration, he showcased his gift right beside the towering anniversary cake for all to see. His unusual gift was a monetary certificate dedicated to building a church in their honor in one of the nations. I call this most appropriate gift an *alignment of catalytic giving*. That is when you hit the sweet spot by giving a gift that is in harmony with the greatest delight of the recipient of the gift.

Pit could not have given a more exceptional gift in his parents' honor. Remembering that every ICM church established in the nations covenants to "pay it forward" by building five daughter churches, this gift is a catalytic investment that will continue giving indefinite returns on the initial investment for eternal benefits. And getting reports on new returns on your investment over the years is just good, old-fashioned fun.

A CATALYTIC LEGACY

During the years of my involvement as development officer with ICM, I have watched thousands of churches being built in many nations of the world as a result of the catalytic giving of many different groups of ordinary believers who have learned the extraordinary joy of becoming catalytic givers. It is a constant inspiration to me to see how God stirs the hearts of sincere believers to participate in catalytic investments into the nations that reap eternal rewards.

I had an idea personally that I thought would inspire some of my friends to increase their vision for investing in the kingdom purposes. I would sponsor a mission trip. Not just your standard idea of a mission trip. It would be a *legacy trip* for fathers and their sons and/or daughters. The idea was birthed from my deep desire to answer a perplexing question: How does a father transfer not only his wealth but especially his godly values from one generation to the next?

First, I took my young son on a legacy trip to Guatemala. When I returned with the happy report of the memorable time I had shared with my son, they asked me if I could help them provide a legacy trip for their children. So it began.

The basic premise was to sponsor a trip for fathers primarily with their teenage children. International travel is still considered extremely cool by teenagers. It's rare and exotic to tell your friends you are going to visit another country. Such a trip also provides a way to get away from all of the distractions and temptations youth wrestle with in our nation. It provides a moment to de-clutter.

And, a mission trip provides a completely new perspective of the world that is bigger and different from America.

A world ravaged by poverty and other great needs greets the affluent American kid with a shocking new reality. Any nation you visit offers a real chance to touch their hearts with the sadness of the human condition of thousands of people.

Many kids who have participated in missions trips learn to appreciate the advantages that their nation's wealth and their parents have given them. Their participation often opens their hearts to potential opportunities to do something significant to make a difference for hurting people. They see firsthand the need to embrace God's great commission and realize there are tangible ways that they can become involved in fulfilling that commission.

In response to my friends' request for a legacy trip with their children, we planned a mission trip to Guatemala visiting churches throughout the country. We listened to these Christians' testimonies of the miraculous power of God, which was alive and well. We experienced their enthusiastic worship.

The impact of the trip on the lives of this missions team was dramatic. They determined to adopt a church to build in Guatemala. They challenged each other, including their children, to go in 100 percent, giving all they had to make this church a reality. Everyone would sacrifice; everyone would give; everyone would participate to make this project "ours." The power of catalytic giving that was released was amazing. Think about a teenager coming up with one hundred or two hundred dollars, which represented every dime they had. Joyfully, without any sense of duty, they reveled in the sense of ownership they had by being a part of this legacy project.

I call it *catalytic legacy giving*—multi-generational giving, the transferring of not only funds but of godly generational values by experiencing firsthand the joy of investing into the kingdom of God. These legacy trips helped me to answer my question regarding transferring my values to my children.

When there is first a catalytic giving of vision, there inevitably follows a catalytic giving of money and other life resources. If you do not want to give your children an inheritance, only to have it them waste it on selfish living, I encourage you to utilize this tool of legacy trips. They are a wonderful way to inspire the next generation to make a difference in the world and to let youth experience the joy of giving to those less fortunate. Combined with sharing the gospel in tangible ways and realizing the potential for making significant investments into the lives of others, these life-changing trips have given godly direction to many youth who have decided to invest their lives into the kingdom of God.

The Joy of Catalytic Living

My friend, Dr. Gills, author of this book, has honored my request to share from my perspective some of the impact of his catalytic investment in ICM church building. I believe it will help his readers to understand that the wonderful truths he is presenting in this book about joyful, catalytic living for God are not mere theory; they are a lifestyle and spiritual reality to the author that have served to focus his generous philanthropic giving throughout our nation and many others for greater spiritual impact.

When Dr. Gills discovered Dois Rosser and ICM, he wanted all his friends to know about the catalytic investment model for Christian missions that could make one donor dollar do the work of five or six dollars. Since then, he has had a major role in funding the building of the thousands of churches in the nations we described earlier. Dr. Gills, with his wife, Heather, have honored scores of their friends and partners by personally building a church and dedicating it in their name.

CATALYTIC MARKETING

In his love for leveraging every donor dollar to maximize its return, Dr. Gills is perhaps the most generous matching giver and the most passionate strategic giver I know personally. When we first met and were discussing a matching gift he was offering, he said, "I never want to do anything by myself. I want to use my charitable giving to encourage others to give. It is not healthy for me to solely support a project."

For Dr. Gills, catalytic investment includes recruiting, enlisting, and empowering others to grasp the vision and network together for synergistic results in kingdom building. In his passionate promotion of ICM and his other Christian philanthropic endeavors, he has acted as a catalyst himself, which we defined as "an agent that provokes or speeds significant change or action in society."[3]

For example, Dr. Gills has introduced pastors to this ministry by inviting them to accompany him on "vision trips" to the nations. Dr. Gills considers this strategic investment in potential partners part of his catalytic giving that will produce more potential for a greater harvest of souls. I call this strategy *catalytic marketing*.

In addition, Dr. Gills has ignited his friends' interest in catalytic giving by sponsoring golf tournaments, house parties, club parties, and gala events around the focus of catalytic, philanthropic investment to affect spiritual as well as social change. He involves study groups and Sunday school classes in discussions of stewardship in giving, which informs and inspires people to join together for catalytic investment.

He introduces his personal friends to the founder of ICM, our friend, Dois Rosser. He also promotes ICM projects through his ophthalmic hospitals and clinics daily by playing a video of our far-flung outreaches. In addition, Dr. Gills places our business cards in his lobby and distributes thousands of our books *gratis*.

While many philanthropists offer generous matching gifts with certain parameters and requirements, the Gills offer capless matches to be determined by the church or group raising the matching funds. I call this *the ultimate catalytic matching model.* These kinds of generous givers undoubtedly reap the greatest returns by challenging others to go all-in and give their best for receiving greater eternal rewards.

Perhaps the greatest accolade we could give to anyone is to call them a servant of God. To become a servant of God fulfills our Savior's definition of greatness: "And whosoever of you will be the chiefest, shall be servant of all" (Mark 10:44, kjv). It is this quality of humility that I see in Dr. and Mrs. Gills that is most endearing and admirable.

You name it; they have done it in their indefatigable efforts to inspire others to make a significant impact for spiritual and social change in the nations, including our own. In my opinion, there is no one who lives a more catalytic lifestyle than the Doc, with his lovely wife, Heather. They are all-in. I call their focused passion for souls the *catalytic life lived.* Out of their deep love for God and for others, they have become servants who are as effective as possible for God's eternal purposes.

Others

Lord, help me live from day to day
In such a self-forgetful way
That even when I kneel to pray
My prayer shall be for—Others.

Refrain:

Others, Lord, yes others,
Let this my motto be,
Help me to live for others,
That I may live like Thee.

Help me in all the work I do
To ever be sincere and true
And know that all I'd do for You
Must needs be done for—Others.

And when my work on earth is done
And my new work in Heavn's begun,
May I forget the crown I've won,
While thinking still of—Others.[1]

And whosoever of you will be the chiefest, shall be servant of all.

—Mark 10:44

Chapter 5

ELEVATED TO SERVANTHOOD

*I tell you when the Spirit of God is on us for service, resting
upon us, we are anointed, and then we can do great things.*

—D L Moody[2]

━━━━◦◦◦◦━━━━

CHARLES COLSON, WHOSE successful career in secular politics led him to the White House as a senior presidential aide to President Richard Nixon, ended in spectacular failure during Watergate.[3] Politically known as "the Hatchet Man" for the president, Charles relished the title as he connived to carry out many dirty tricks for Nixon's administration. Colson's ruthlessness was symbolized in an internal memo he wrote with the line, "I would walk over my grandmother for Richard Nixon."[4]

So, when scandal broke, the press and prosecutors pursued Colson, knowing he was a major contributor to the unsavory moral climate inside the White House. Colson later admitted that he had no moral compass for the first forty-one years of his life. He told one interviewer who questioned him about his faith, "Oh, I think religion is fine, provided one has as little of it as possible."[5]

Soon after Colson left the White House and was attempting to rebuild his career as a lawyer, he made an appointment with Tom Phillips, the chief executive of Raytheon. He was unaware that Phillips had recently come to Christ at a Billy Graham rally. Colson's aim was to land some of Raytheon's legal business. Instead, he had to listen to Phillips talk with passion about his newfound faith, reading to him lengthy passages from *Mere Christianity* by C S Lewis.

The words from Lewis's chapter on pride, called "The Great Sin," struck home in Charles Colson's mind and heart. So did the prayer Tom Phillips prayed for him at the end of their meeting, asking Jesus Christ "to open Chuck's heart and show him the light and the way."[6] On his way home that night, Colson broke down in tears at the wheel of his car and offered a prayer of his own. As he climbed into bed, he told his wife, Patty, that he thought he'd had a conversion experience—though he did not know what the term meant.

Tom Phillips connected Chuck with godly mentors and other believers in a small prayer group. They became a support group for him during the unfolding Watergate scandal, which resulted in Colson's ultimate prosecution and conviction. These caring, Christian brothers became Colson's lifeline of spiritual support during this devastating time in his life.

Though there was little evidence against him regarding the actual Watergate scandal, rejecting his lawyer's advice, Colson chose to plead guilty on a legal technicality. In the fevered atmosphere of Watergate, a judge accepted his guilty plea and sentenced Colson to a one- to three-year prison term.

THE CATALYTIC POWER OF PERSONAL REDEMPTION

It was during his time in jail that Colson began to learn difficult spiritual lessons regarding humility, penitence, and forgiveness. Disappointments and loss bombarded him. He did not receive the presidential pardon he was expecting after the clemency granted to Nixon. He was disbarred from practicing law. And he suffered personal loss of the death of his father, along with his son's arrest for narcotics possession.

But, as Chuck immersed himself in Bible reading and prayer, he began to discover the liberating power of *coram Deo*—living before the face of God. He became aware of the men in the prison around him who seemingly did not know the love of God he had found so comforting and which sustained him. Allowing the Spirit of God to fill his heart with compassion for his fellow prisoners, he started a prayer group with them.

As they say—the rest is history. That first prayer group would culminate in a worldwide outreach to thousands of prisons through Colson's Prison Fellowship (PF). After serving seven months of his sentence, Chuck was paroled. Still a new believer, he was following a new passion for helping fellow prisoners come to know Christ.

Though he continued to struggle with personal issues of his faith,

God's plan for his life and future was becoming clearer. He initiated the idea of creating a discipleship program for prisoners, who would be furloughed to a Christian retreat house. Reluctantly, the head of the Federal Bureau of Prisons, Norman Carlson, agreed to the idea on an experimental basis. This was the genesis of what was to develop into the worldwide ministry of Prison Fellowship.

While pursuing his new vocation for discipling prisoners, Colson wrote the book *Born Again,* which became a worldwide bestseller. In that book, Chuck candidly shared a searingly emotional narrative about his life journey and his conversion to Christ. Selling over three million copies, it catapulted him into the stratosphere of being a "celebrity Christian." Colson rejected the label as a dangerous oxymoron, contradicting the requisite quality of humility and servanthood that should lie at the heart of every Christian's godly witness.

With his formidable energy and passion for sharing the love of God with others, Chuck Colson would discover the power of catalytic giving as he networked with like-minded friends. Again, this passionate caregiver's legacy is outliving him today, since his death in 2012. Prison Fellowship is flourishing today in over one hundred and twenty countries.

Within the United States, PF launched powerful programs like Justice Fellowship, advocating for restorative justice policies and laws; Angel Tree, delivering Christmas gifts and the gospel message to hundreds of thousands of children to prisoners; and extensive in-prison ministry and pre-release programs to help bring hope and healing to the incarcerated. Charles continued to be a prolific author, publishing over twenty books, and became a successful broadcaster on his own weekly radio program, *BreakPoint.*

God had miraculously elevated Charles Colson from having a vengeful demeanor and unsavory political goals to a purpose-filled stature of servanthood. His godly influence has touched millions of lives through his writings and his international outreach through Prison Fellowship and related programs. He received numerous awards recognizing his achievements as a Christian leader and apologist, one of the most prestigious being the 1993 Templeton Prize for Religion. The 1 million dollars he was awarded with that prize, he donated to charity.

Personal Connection

It is an honor for me to call Chuck Colson my friend. One of the catalytic connections we pursued was his helping me to distribute the inspirational writings I had published during my journey into intimate relationship with God. As I became more filled with God's love for others, I began to share His love through the publication of inspirational novels and thematic writings.

Sometimes through the troubled characters in a novel who discovered peace through relationship with Christ and other times addressing specific life issues, I began to make the spiritual insight I had received of the reality of Christ's joy-filled living available to all believers. To distribute these inspirational books, I founded Love Press, a non-profit publishing arm that began by placing of these books *gratis* into hospitals, doctors' offices, and other public facilities. It is our hope that people will take them home and receive spiritual insight to help them walk in God's divine love.

Then, when I crossed paths with Charles Colson and His Prison Fellowship ministry, I suggested we distribute these materials to the inmates as well. Through Chuck's influence, we were able to overcome political and other barriers and placed these books into the hands of precious incarcerated men and women. This synergism of our efforts ignited the principle of catalytic giving, allowing us share the gospel in jails and prisons in every state in the United States, including every death row facility.

Our office receives letters weekly from chaplains and other prison officials, as well as grateful incarcerated men and women who are receiving the truth of the gospel for the first time through these books. It gives us indescribable joy to read these letters and witness the evidence of the grace of God working in their lives. For example:

> Dear Dr. Gills,
>
> Thank you for your continued support of incarcerated men. While imprisoned many of these men find strength and renewed faith while reading *Believe and Rejoice* and other Christian materials. They take this book with them to their permanent institution for continued [inspiration].
>
> —Chaplain, Washington Correction Center

Dr. James P. Gills,

I am currently awaiting my trial and have been incarcerated for nine months. I picked up your book *The Prayerful Spirit,* only because of the eagle on the cover. There is a prayer in your book that I have memorized and wrote down for many inmates to help them out during our difficult times. I say this prayer every day, many times. It is a reminder the Lord is with me. I can honestly say I am a sinner and have asked our Lord for His forgiveness.

—Ella

Dear Brother James,

I am the chaplain at Tucker Correctional Unit, where we serve close to a thousand men and women. We have requests for your books *Tender Journey* and *Love: Fulfilling the Ultimate Quest.* Thank you for allowing us to be partners with you in reaching out and touching the hearts of these men and women.

—Chaplain, Tucker, Arkansas

Dear Love Press,

My name is Judy...and I am a pastor's daughter. I have read three of your books already and will be starting on the fourth one tonight. Your books have given me deeper bonding with the Lord and a more clear walk with Him. Things I didn't understand before, I have a better understanding of now. I would like to read more of your books if possible.

—Suffolk, VA

Editor's Note

During the preparation of materials for this manuscript, I discovered a powerful, little-known story of friendship and catalytic giving involving Jack Eckerd and Dr. Gills. They became aware of a critical financial crisis facing Chuck Colson's Prison Fellowship. These friends assessed the need and, deeming this effective Christian outreach to thousands of incarcerated people worthy of their investment, each man donated one hundred and twenty-five thousand dollars.

That investment would become a catalytic gift through matching funds that Chuck Colson received to resolve the financial challenge that threatened the existence of PF. As a result of that investment, Prison Fellowship received 1.8 million dollars, which resolved the crisis. And PF is going strong today in over 120 countries.

Though modesty does not permit Dr. Gills to reveal such stories of his charitable giving to spread the gospel, I was given the liberty to share it with the reader that you might understand his personal commitment to the truths he is sharing and in turn be inspired by these examples of catalytic giving, as I have been.

Blessings.

—CAROL NOE, EDITOR

GOOD WORKS OF A SERVANT HEART

Many of Charles Colson's fellow Christians say about him, "God changed Charles Colson and used him for good." His powerful testimony of personal redemption that led to his entirely new vocation in life is still having catalytic impact worldwide in for the gospel of Christ.

Amazing grace! God intends that all believers enjoy this kind of purpose-filled living through cultivating an intimate relationship with Him and then walking in the good works He created us to do. The apostle Paul declared the reality of walking in our God-ordained purpose as a servant of good works:

> For by grace are ye saved through faith; and that not of ourselves: it is the gift of God: Not of works, lest any man should boast. For we are his workmanship, created in Christ Jesus unto good works, which God hath before ordained that we should walk in them.
>
> —EPHESIANS 2:8–10, KJV

Those "good works" that God has ordained for us will inevitably lead us into a life of fulfillment we could not possibly realize in our own singular efforts. As we submit to the Holy Spirit and allow Him to *elevate* us to the echelon of servanthood, we will discover divine connections with others with whom we can network our lives and purposes. Our shared catalytic investment will reap a wonderful harvest of souls as we share the love of God with others who do not know Him.

Extreme Redemption

Most people are familiar with the somewhat overused term *extreme,* as it is applied to daring sports and other intense, high-energy, risk-filled ventures. Have you considered applying the term *extreme* to the phenomena of Christ's redemption of lives whose stories we have discussed? Mother Teresa, Dois Rosser, Dick Woodward, Willie Hunter, Juan Batlle, Chuck Colson, and others like them represent lives and character radically transformed by the work of the Spirit in their hearts. As they have allowed the extreme redemption of God's Spirit to empower them through living a lifestyle of *coram Deo,* they have become living demonstrations of the divine love of God.

Each, through their personal giftings and in their sphere of life, have brought glory to God through their humble posture of extreme servanthood. Out of their passion for intimate relationship with their Lord flowed their love for others, resulting in the amazing good works for sharing His love that God had ordained for each of them. Their lives reflect the beautiful reality that in knowing Christ intimately His love empowers us to do greater works than we could imagine in fulfilling God's divine purpose for our lives.

It is in the divine light of His presence that we begin to comprehend the profound reality of the Westminster Catechism's tenet for the purpose of mankind: "Man's chief end is to glorify God and enjoy Him forever."[7] John Piper adds this paraphrase to this foundational truth: "It is in enjoying God that we bring glory to Him."[8]

If you live gladly to make others glad in God, your life will be hard, your risks will be high, and your joy will be full.

—JOHN PIPER[1]

Chapter 6

INSPIRED BY GENEROUS GIVERS, INC.

~&~

G ENEROSITY IS A virtue that is, of course, not limited to monetary giving. As we have discussed, catalytic giving encompasses every area of the human experience. There are many ways to give of our lives to make a positive impact on the well-being of others. Some people have devoted their time and energies to helping the homeless, the widows, those who are incarcerated, as well as at-risk children and youth. Others have established orphanages in other nations to care for precious children who would otherwise live and die on the streets, desperately fending for themselves.

There are Christians whose others-centered lives are engaged in the loving ministry of combating human trafficking, rescuing precious souls sometimes at the risk of their own lives. They help children and young women escape their masters, who violate their victims in unthinkable ways.

There are others who work tirelessly in outreaches to counsel pregnant women, helping them understand the blessing of choosing life. They are preventing the inevitable guilt and shame of mothers, as well as saving the lives of the unborn.

Centers for rehabilitation of people who suffer drug and alcohol addictions, depression, and other destructive lifestyles are giving hope to many who seek freedom from these afflictions.

And always, countless people who are giving to help feed the poor among us alleviate much suffering for young and old alike. In these and myriad other ways, people seek opportunities to love their neighbor as themselves.

It is a simple fact that each person can offer some kind of help to another person when motivated by the love of God to do so. Even a smile of acceptance and encouragement can make a difference for a child or adult who is struggling with life's painful challenges. As we have seen, it is in cultivating a mind-set motivated by encountering the extravagant love of God—by which we begin to see others through the divine lens of a generous, caring heart—that compels us to give to others.

What Defines Success?

It was a great challenge to me as a young man to understand what motivated people to succeed and to what meaningful purpose they lived their lives. I observed people who were wealthy by the world's standards and wondered why they were obviously discontent, living unfulfilled lives while amassing great wealth.

Others I observed had successfully attained a great measure of wealth and were obviously filled with joy in living. I sensed they were not infatuated with their "stuff" but were enjoying great fulfillment in living the purpose for their lives. I couldn't help contrasting these two very different states of mind—the discontent and the joyful—among people who enjoyed the same successful financial status.

I had to ask the hard question, Which kind of person do you want to be? One who is wealthy in worldly goods, fame, or social standing who owes a million dollars to the government when they die, or one who is wealthy in God's blessing and favor, infused with the joy and fulfillment of purpose-filled living?

Then I began to notice that the successful people who were filled with joy were those who had found a spiritual richness in life through their relationship with God. They were genuinely embracing the Word of God for their lives, pursuing His purposes and enjoying the fulfillment they had discovered in giving to others.

Some of these joy-filled people actually gave away more than they earned. They found fulfillment in living a generous life that did not end after their prime working years were finished. Their passion for others compelled them to give to others the riches they had earned but knew they could not take out of this world. I saw that their giving was focused on helping others realize the eternal riches of peace with God.

Wise Thoughts from a Philanthropist

Sheila Johnson was born on January 25, 1949, in McKeesport, Pennsylvania. She co-founded Black Entertainment Television (BET) in 1979. The successful station focused on African-American audiences and was sold to Viacom for 3 billion dollars in 2002. Johnson is currently part-owner of sports teams, including the Washington Capitals (NHL), the Washington Wizards (NBA), and the Washington Mystics (WNBA) and is the second wealthiest black female in the United States.[2]

As a gifted entrepreneur, accomplished musician, and philanthropist, Sheila became America's first black billionairess. In an interview with Kam Williams, she was asked, "What do you want to be remembered for?"[3] I like her response: "As a woman who was always generous, not only with her pocketbook, but with her heart." Then when asked what her fans could do to help her, she replied, "By, instead of asking for a handout, offering to help me help others."

In spite of all her brilliant achievements, Sheila simply wants to be remembered as a generous person, one who cultivated the virtue of a caring heart. She really understands how important it is to give to others and has done a beautiful job exemplifying a woman who has developed into a great businesswoman who focuses her priority on being a generous philanthropist.

I have heard it said that early in life you grab; later in life your hand opens and you give. Maturity changes our perspective of the true values of life. As you mature, you find yourself discarding the immaturity of grabbing and exchanging it for the much more satisfying life perspective of giving to make a difference for others. That is especially true for all who pursue a personal relationship with our heavenly Father, who shows us His extravagant, giving love in the gift of life itself.

Generous Giving, Inc.

I have great admiration for a unique Christian organization called Generous Giving, Inc., whose purpose is to motivate followers of Jesus Christ toward a lifestyle of biblical generosity. Their message proclaims the joy of giving we experience out of gratitude for salvation in Christ. They believe that generosity is God's message for all followers of Christ and that generous giving is to be motivated by joy, primarily in response to the grace we have received rather than out of dutiful obedience. While it is God, through His Word and the ministry of the Holy Spirit, who brings transformation, we can be used as tools in facilitating opportunities for God's Word to be heard and the Holy Spirit to transform lives as a result.[4]

Based on the biblical tenet that God is the rightful owner of everything (Ps. 24:1), Generous Giving, Inc., is a privately funded ministry that hosts retreats and conferences to encourage and teach stewardship as a lifestyle. Their simple message is that we are caretakers of God's world, responsible to do with it what He wants done. While there are many aspects of stewardship, the Bible frequently singles out financial generosity as the one most representative of a person's heart (Matt. 6:19–21).

The organization was launched in 2000 by the Maclellan Foundation to stir a renewed, Spirit-led commitment to generosity among Christians. It does not solicit donations. These dedicated, financially successful Christians have found the reality of God's desire for us to be filled with joy and to bring Him glory through embracing the truth of God's Word for our lives, especially regarding catalytic giving.

Leaders of Generous Giving, Inc., believe that generosity is one of the chief evidences in a Christian's life that he or she truly knows and loves God. Our gratitude for His redemptive love can best be expressed by sharing that love with others. It reflects our maturity as sons and daughters of God when our greatest desire is to please our Father's heart by stewarding our finances in biblical ways to promote the kingdom of God.

Avoiding the Destructive Love of Money

Living for ourselves, seeking only what we can get or achieve personally, simply does not compare with the joy of living a purpose-filled life, which Jesus came to give to us. Defining success in life as Jesus defines it mandates that we learn to love God with our whole heart and to share His love with others. This godly worldview will keep us from the discontent and self-destructions that await those who seek for satisfaction in lesser things. The apostle Paul gave advice to the young man, Timothy, which is as timely today as it was then:

> Godliness actually is a means of great gain when accompanied by contentment. For we have brought nothing into the world, so we cannot take anything out of it either. If we have food and covering, with these we shall be content. But those who want to get rich fall into temptation and a snare and many foolish and harmful desires which plunge men into ruin and destruction. For the love of money is a root of all sorts of evil.
>
> —1 TIMOTHY 6:6–10, NASB

Heeding this advice regarding our relationship to money and material success will bring divine blessing to our life, our family, our community, and even our nation. It is not a negative to want to make money; prosperity is a wonderful tool for giving opportunity to reach out to others with God's love

According to the Scriptures, it is simply imperative that you avoid the destructive power the *love* of money can have over your life. It is not money, but the love of it, according to the Scriptures, that brings destruction. The love of money will infect your life with greed if you use it simply to satisfy your own selfish goals.

It is that greed that spawns many evils on every level, from individuals to international woes. You are probably aware that the love of money causes people to steal and cheat, to marry for devious motives, and even to develop a lifestyle of extortion. For good reason the Bible calls the love of money the root of all evils.

This egotistical pursuit of financial gain causes people to wander from true faith and end up with a life of misery. Paul said that godliness is the key to happiness. There is simply no contentment to be found, no matter your financial wealth, if your life (and your wealth) is not abandoned to the purposes of God.

Jesus taught that to whom much is given, from him much will be required, and to whom much has been committed, of him they will ask the more (Luke 12:48). As I look at people I know who give away more than they earn, I see those who have been given much without falling captive to greed. Most often, they are older, mature Christians who realize that true joy is found in giving; they understand the truth of the Scriptures that "it is more blessed to give than to receive" (Acts 20:35, NASB). Their lives reflect the wisdom of Jesus when He declared,

"He who is faithful in what is least is faithful also in much" (Luke 16:10, NKJV).

The converse of Jesus' statement is also true for those who fail to embrace a generous spirit: "And he who is unjust in what is least is unjust also in much" (Luke 16:10, NKJV). That understanding reveals the importance of our choosing to give to those who cannot give back and helping those who have the greatest need, no matter how small the amount we have to give.

Where the Word of God is embraced and the love of God fills hearts, we see generous spirits looking for meaningful ways to give to others, whether in monetary ways or service opportunities, or both. We rarely see it otherwise. Only in the light of God's Word, through a work of the Spirit in our hearts, can we begin to desire to fulfill His divine purpose for the generous dispensing of our personal wealth.

In the apostle Paul's advice to the young man Timothy, he states what should be the obvious—that we brought nothing into the world, and we cannot take anything out of the world (1 Tim. 6:7). He points Timothy to the true source of abundant wealth: "godliness [accompanied] with contentment" (v. 6, NKJV). That wonderful truth makes it possible for the poorest among us to enjoy the true wealth of living a godly life, experiencing the contentment possible only in intimate relationship with God. That, in turn, will usher us into the divine blessing of a purpose-filled life and the joy of giving to others in every opportunity we are given. (Please see Appendix C for biblical promises for giving.)

Profound Warning

In Paul's discourse with Timothy on the proper perspective regarding money, he issues a rather ominous warning for those who do not heed the injunction. Because the love of money is the root of all evil (remember, not money itself but the *love* of it), Paul warns, "For which some have strayed from the faith in their greediness, and pierced themselves through with many sorrows" (1 Tim. 6:10, NKJV).

I am fairly confident that you know someone or at least know of someone who has done just that as a result of their faulty worldview of wealth. Personal tragedy often results from indulging in the destructive sin of greed through selfishly hoarding their wealth for ungodly purposes.

The Scriptures are filled with admonitions and warnings regarding our relationship with and motivation toward getting money and desiring riches:

> He who is of a proud heart stirs up strife, But he who trusts in the LORD will be prospered.
>
> —PROVERBS 28:25, NKJV

> He who loves silver will not be satisfied with silver; Nor he who loves abundance, with increase. This also is vanity.
>
> —ECCLESIASTES 5:10, NKJV

> You can't worship two gods at once. Loving one god, you'll end up hating the other. Adoration of one feeds contempt for the other. You can't worship God and Money both.
>
> —MATTHEW 6:24, THE MESSAGE

> Keep your lives free from the love of money, and be content with what you have; for he has said, "I will never leave you or forsake you."
>
> —HEBREWS 13:5

> Shepherd the flock of God which is among you, serving as overseers, not by compulsion but willingly, not for dishonest gain but eagerly.
>
> —1 PETER 5:2, NKJV

Becoming mature sons and daughters of our heavenly Father involves surrendering every aspect of our lives to fulfill His will. As we wait on God and embrace the truth of His Word, the Spirit of God works a wonderful metamorphosis in our hearts, changing us from self-centered creatures into loving people who are focused on serving others. There simply is no greater joy or sense of fulfillment in life than knowing you are accomplishing the good works that Christ ordained for your life.

Spread love everywhere you go. Let no one ever come to you without leaving happier.

—Mother Teresa[1]

Chapter 7

FULFILLING YOUR DESTINY

———⌘———

A s you have read the stories of joy-filled, catalytic givers who are impacting nations with the good news of the gospel, I wonder if you have asked yourself the question, *Am I a giver or a taker?* Perhaps after reading through these chapters you are more ready to give an honest answer to yourself, first of all, and then to God. Have you detected selfishness or greed in your heart that makes you cling to things and always want more?

Or do you genuinely desire to cultivate a lifestyle of *coram Deo*—living before the face of God—and allow Him to catapult you into your joyful and purpose-filled destiny? Do you want your life to have greater spiritual impact for touching the lives of others with the love of God you have received?

Whatever your present heart condition or perspective of life, you can receive the grace of God to cleanse you of self-centeredness and transform your life to look more like those you have read about in these pages. You can experience the joy and love of God they have known as they have allowed the work of the Spirit in their lives to lead them into catalytic connections and personal fulfillment of divine purpose.

Life, both natural and spiritual, is a journey. It begins with birth, then continues through a transforming process to maturity. When a baby is born we understand that it will take years of physical growth, nurturing, education, and life experiences before he or she will reach mature adulthood. This complex, sometimes painful, process involves living every moment of every day. It requires the help of responsible adults cultivating age-appropriate environments in order for us to move from infancy to childhood to healthy, mature adulthood.

I have found that this natural journey is analogous to our spiritual growth process in becoming mature sons and daughters in Christ. During my lifelong spiritual journey as a born-again Christian, I have endured the complexities and painful experiences involved in becoming a mature son of God. I have realized my need for continually nurturing an intimate relationship with God, as well as for the godly mentoring of pastors and friends to encourage me in my journey.

Living every moment of every day with a desire to please God is requisite to developing an ever-enlarging Christian worldview, along with godly attitudes, motivations, and desires. Waiting daily in His presence in prayer, learning to embrace the truth of His Word, and receiving His grace to face difficult life situations—*coram Deo*—are all-important aspects of our spiritual maturation process. It is there that we find the joy of discovering God's purpose for our lives, which is key to promoting our growth to maturity as sons and daughters of God. (Please see Appendix B for biblical references to relationship with God.)

Maturity in Godly Character

The apostle Paul taught that, as believers, we were not to remain like children in our walk with Christ. He admonishes us that "we all come in the unity of the faith, and of the knowledge of the Son of God, to a perfect man, to the measure of the stature of the fullness of Christ" (Eph. 4:13, nkjv), and that "speaking the truth in love, [we] may grow up in all things into Him who is the head—Christ" (v. 15).

Maturity in godly character is reflected in the development of godly motivations and desires, which are given to us through the work of the Spirit in our lives. This spiritual growth does not happen automatically simply because we are born-again Christians. It requires continual nurturing of healthy appetites for prayer, for the study of the Word of God, and for fellowship with the body of Christ.

The journey to maturity in Christ is a fascinating, sometimes arduous journey. It requires that we allow the Spirit of God to develop in us the Christian character and godly love revealed in the lives of believers throughout the Scriptures. The spiritual DNA of people of faith whose lives are recorded in the Bible reflected their love for God and desire to please Him. In their emotional responses, relationships, activities, and every facet of life, they embraced the purpose-filled life they saw in obeying the commandments of God and in the obedience of their Savior, Jesus Christ.

At times it is difficult to overcome the human tendency to fear, selfishness, ingratitude, and other aspects of spiritual darkness lurking in our souls. But as believers, when we continually embrace the reality of living faith in Christ, the Spirit enlarges our desire for a *coram Deo* lifestyle. As we spend time with Him alone daily, He empowers us to lay aside lesser things in order to "win Christ" and to fulfill His purpose for our lives (Phil. 3:8). We begin to understand the passion of the apostle Paul, who wrote:

> I count all things but loss for the excellency of the knowledge of Christ Jesus my Lord: for whom I have suffered the loss of all things, and do count them but dung, that I may win Christ, And be found in him, not having mine own righteousness...but that which is through the faith of Christ.
>
> —PHILIPPIANS 3:8–9, KJV

Laying aside my goals, interests, and desires is not always easy. But when compared to the joy and fulfillment I have found in walking in intimate relationship with my Creator–Redeemer, the value of those things pales in comparison to His love filling my heart. This revelation of life in God's kingdom, attended by the Spirit's work in my heart, has filled me with a wonder that transcends every earthly desire.

FULFILLING OUR STATEMENT OF MISSION

Now, as I am enjoying my seventh decade of my journey with God, I rejoice that the continuing work of the Spirit in my life has increasingly cleansed the selfishness of my heart, filling me with ever greater joy and a deep desire to share God's love with as many people as we can reach. As I stated earlier, we have focused our energies and efforts through our medical and philanthropic enterprises to fulfill this simple statement of mission:

> To be a catalyst for Jesus Christ by giving the inspired Word of God to the souls of people and mentoring them to spiritual maturity.[2]

To reiterate our purpose in the more personal terms of my friend and colleague, Pastor Gary Carter, it is:

To daily possess for myself and then transfer to others the joy, awe, wonder, and satisfaction of knowing the Son of God in saving communion by the word of God, prayer, and the loving service of others in dependence upon the Holy Spirit's power.

Perhaps one of the most defining features of humanity is our capacity for empathy—the ability to put ourselves in others' shoes. As disciples of Christ, we are always learning the spiritual reality of experiencing true empathy with people who do not know Him.

Mother Teresa said, "If we have no peace, it is because we have forgotten that we belong to each other."[3] Our mission statement mandates that we accept that spiritual reality and that we be catalysts to inspire others to live the abundant, purpose-filled life found only in serving Jesus Christ. We understand that we can only succeed in this task through the ongoing work of the Spirit in our lives. To that end we give ourselves to the daily study of the Word of God and to fervent prayer, pursuing a relationship with Him.

God has filled my heart with a determination to become a mature son of God, sharing in the extravagant love of His heart, which is not willing for any to perish but desires that all people come to know His redemptive love (2 Pet. 3:9). I have discovered that getting to know God intimately is to experience, in a small measure, His infinite love for all of humanity and, it follows, to discover the profound joy that comes from sharing that love with others.

> If we have no peace, it is because we have forgotten that we belong to each other.
> —Mother Teresa[4]

No Retirement Strategy

Now, living beyond normal retirement age, I am realizing that if I am to fulfill our stated mission, there can simply be no retirement strategy. The ever-expanding doors that are opening to us through medical missions and other mission outreaches require that we continue to work hard in our ophthalmic profession simply to meet our commitments to support these exciting spiritual enterprises. Such a mandate requires a continually growing trust in God to provide every need "according to His riches in...Christ Jesus" (Phil. 4:19, KJV).

When friends and family ask why we insist on giving so extensively of our resources to help those in need, I can only try to describe the passion in my heart for sharing the love of God with desperate people. The profound impact of His love in my life and the joy it brings motivates me to reach others with His love. It inspires my own heart to continually look for open doors to reach more people with the good news of Christ's redemption.

THE AMAZING PROVIDENCE OF GOD

It is increasingly amazing to me, when I look back on my life journey, to see how the loving hand of God in His sovereignty has guided my life pursuits. I now understand that it is the way of God to work first *in* a man or woman to prepare their hearts so He can pour His love *through* them to impact the lives of others.

I was not aware, as a young medical student, that God had a far greater purpose for my medical studies as part of His sovereign plan for my life. Through the years, He has continually transformed my way of thinking, my perspective, and goals as He continually reveals to me the greater purpose He has for my life.

My life story is a testimony to the grace of God, which turned the heart of a young scientist from primarily pursuing personal goals to finding a purpose-filled life in Christ, focused on serving others. I could not imagine the joy I would experience in discovering providential relationships with other like-minded men and women and through catalytic giving, being empowered together to fulfill His purpose for our lives and enjoy the ultimate satisfaction God gives in sharing His love with others.

Yet, life in Christ does not preclude difficulties, disappointments, failures, and sorrows, as we saw in the exemplary, godly life of our friend, Dick Woodward. Jesus promised we would have tribulation in the world but gave us the assurance that He has overcome the world (John 16:33). He promises that we can be more than conquerors as we pursue a life of *coram Deo* and find the fulfillment of purpose He gives to us.

No matter what painful situations we face in life, they become manageable when we learn to trust them to God. As our trust in our loving heavenly Father deepens, we receive inspiration from those very difficulties to trust Him more rather than allowing them to discourage and defeat our life of faith in God.

For me, the key to triumphing over life's troubles has been learning to live before the face of God—*coram Deo*—in daily worship and communion with Him in prayer and in the Scriptures. Choosing a lifestyle of humbling ourselves before God in worship allows the work of the Spirit to fill our lives with His righteousness, peace, and joy. In that intimate love relationship, God fills us with desire to live purpose-filled lives focused on sharing His divine love with others.

As members of the body of Christ, we begin to live adventure-filled lives. We learn to network together as catalytic givers, every joint and ligament supplying, to impact the world for the kingdom of God. This servant lifestyle represents true greatness, according to our Lord (Matt. 20:27), and allows us to fulfill our divine purpose, for which we were born.

I am convinced that allowing the work of the Spirit to nurture us to becoming mature sons and daughters of God is the answer to living a life of joy beyond belief. In choosing to live a servant lifestyle as catalytic givers in the body of Christ, He gives us a godly cry: "Thy kingdom come...in earth, as it is in heaven" (Matt. 6:10, kjv). And He is faithful to answer that cry in allowing us to reap a harvest of souls for Christ.

TRIBUTE TO AN EXCEPTIONAL SERVANT OF GOD

❦

A s I wrote the final pages of this book, I had to say good-bye to my friend and colleague, Dick Woodward. A phenomenal example of *Discover the Joy of Catalytic Giving—For Christ*, whose godly life and friendship deeply impacted my life, Dick was ushered into his heavenly reward on March, 8, 2014.

Without a doubt, he has heard His Savior say, "Well done, thou good and faithful servant…enter thou into the joy of the Lord" (Matt. 25:21). While we mourn the loss of this amazing example of a mature son of God, we must also rejoice with him in his home-going, for he has seen his Savior face to face and entered into his eternal reward. We find comfort in the hope we share of spending eternity together in our Lord's presence.

You will remember that Dick Woodward's *Mini Bible College* has been translated into dozens of languages (with more coming) and has reached into scores of nations as the Bible curriculum used to mentor precious converts around the world. In spite of his physical limitations, Dick embodied the lifestyle of spiritual catalytic investment, not only of his teaching of the Word but in counseling, mentoring, and in countless other ways.

At Dick's memorial service, hundreds of people came to pay tribute to their friend, mentor, pastor, and colleague in ministry.[1] His son, Dean Woodward, himself a pastor, eulogized his father on behalf of the family. He spoke lovingly and tenderly of the Christlike man who was his father. He gave tribute to the man who had so characterized the heavenly father that his children, grandchildren, and great-grandchildren desired to emulate his life.

Dean Woodward noted that the fruit of the Spirit of *love and joy* were especially predominant in his father's life, which shocked some, who expected to see a depressed, angry, embittered person lying helpless in a hospital bed. (Dick had suffered adult onset of a rare disease that affected the spine, ultimately rendering him a quadriplegic. He was cared for by his loving wife, Ginny).

In spite of his father's full-body paralysis and 24/7 pain, he had so allowed Christ to fill his heart with the fruit of the Spirit that scores of people who came for counsel left feeling that they had been in the presence of God. They had tasted the love and joy of God that radiated from Dick's life.

Yet, the most predominant fruit of the Spirit that was so apparent in Dick Woodward's life was the fruit of *patience*, according to his family. It was not God's punishment that caused the deterioration of Dick's body. In His sovereignty, God had made Dick a living object lesson of the power of divine patience through endurance of extreme affliction.

Those with lesser complaints were humbled in his presence, as they experienced the genuine joy and love of God flowing through Dick's life. He understood that when he ministered the love of God to a needy person, it did not only benefit the person to whom he ministered. As a channel for the love of God, Dick was extremely blessed and comforted in his tribulation.

As a tribute to my friend, whose global influence for the gospel of Christ so effectively embodies the theme of this book, I have included the touching eulogy for Dick Woodward, given by his son, Pastor Dean Woodward, to inspire your hearts toward living a life of catalytic giving. It is simply not humanly possible to evaluate the impact of Dick's life on others this side of eternity. Through the great grace of God, Dick turned the tragic circumstance of his ill health into triumph for the kingdom of God, which these few words regarding his remarkable life only begin to describe:

DICK WOODWARD

October 29, 1930—March 8, 2014[2]

WILLIAMSBURG, Va. — Dick Woodward—cherished pastor, teacher, author, mentor and friend—departed this life on Saturday, March 8. He was 83.

Known to hundreds of thousands of Christians all over

the world as the author of the *Mini Bible College*, a practical survey of the Bible, Woodward began his ministry as an associate pastor at his brother-in-law's church in Norfolk after graduating from Biola University. Initially a shy, angry young man with crippling social anxiety and a learning disability, Woodward seemed an unlikely candidate for a powerful preaching and teaching ministry. He said:

> I spent a good part of my early faith journey as a reluctant, confused, and even rebellious disciple. I have learned, though, how God responds in amazing ways when we humble ourselves and determine to live life as He designed it.

Indeed, "amazing" accurately describes the early years of Woodward's ministry. In 1956, he founded Virginia Beach Community Chapel with twenty members and became its senior pastor. By 1979, it had become a megachurch. Pastor Woodward appeared on the Mildred Alexander talk show and spoke on radio programs and before multiple Bible study groups. A weekly prayer breakfast Woodward had started for local businessmen, known as "The Thursday Morning Happening," had grown to an attendance of 400. He moved to Williamsburg and helped establish a second church, Williamsburg Community Chapel. In the midst of managing such a successful ministry, however, Woodward held a memory of an early encounter he had with God's divine love:

> I discovered where God is... and I discovered where I wanted to be for the rest of my life, connecting the love of God to the pain of hurting people.

Little did Woodward know where this encounter had yet to take him.

By the late 1970s, it was clear something was amiss in Woodward's body. A man who once ran several miles a day now struggled to walk. The doctors came back with devastating news: Woodward had a rare degenerative disease of the spine. By the mid-1980s, he was a paraplegic—by the late 1990s, a housebound, bedfast quadriplegic. To Woodward, it seemed that his vibrant ministry had suddenly ground to a halt.

Instead, it proved to be a new beginning. As his health declined, Woodward began writing and teaching a survey of the Bible designed to help common people grow in their understanding of the Scriptures. He called it the *Mini Bible College.* Dois Rosser, a successful Virginia businessman, found Woodward's approach to the Bible so clear and compelling that he vowed to put the *Mini Bible College* into the hands of people all over the world. Dois founded International Cooperating Ministries, which set to work translating the *Mini Bible College* into various languages for distribution in Asia, Africa, Latin America and Eastern Europe. Today, the *Mini Bible College* exists in thirty-one languages spoken by 4 billion people worldwide and is actively undergoing translation into ten additional ones. MBC is now available on the Internet, solar-powered audio devices and radio broadcast.

Perhaps the most powerful facet of Woodward's ministry, however, was his persistent faith in the face of incredible suffering. Throughout his life and ministry, he continued to pray and believe fervently for the healing of others. He mentored many at his bedside and ministered to the health care providers who attended him in the hospital.

"Somehow, my acceptance [of my condition] was so complete that it washed out the denial, anger, and depression I had felt before. Since the inward person is a greater value than the outward person, inner healing is a greater value than physical healing. I believe God has done a far deeper healing in my soul which few people can see; it's a greater miracle than the healing of my body would be, which everyone could see."

In 2008, Woodward started a blog to share with the

world the lessons of faith that had long since become the foundation of his ministry and the *Mini Bible College*—which he called "the Four Spiritual Secrets." In 2010, he published a book by the same name. Woodward's story has ministered to the hearts of countless people in difficult circumstances, connecting the love of God to the pain of the hurting in a tender, tangible way.

> "God has given me His ability in exchange for my disability," Woodward would often say. "I'm not, but he is. I can't, but He can. I didn't, but He did. I don't want to, but He wants to—because I am in Him and He is in me."

Dick Woodward leaves behind his beloved wife, Ginny, two sons, three daughters, two sons-in-law, one daughter-in-law, five grandchildren and four great-grandchildren.

POWER OF MATCHING AND MULTIPLYING IN INDIA

—∞∞—

POWER OF MATCHING AND MULTIPLYING IN INDIA			
Matching: "Finish the work, so that your eager willingness to do it may be matched by your completion of it, according to your means" (2 Cor. 8:11, NIV).			**Cumulative Impact Becomes**
Matching Investment to Build Mother Church	$1.00	Church Building Donation	$1.00
	50%	Training and Orphanage Match	$1.50
	50%	Matching Gift	$2.25
	150%	Partnership In-Country Contribution (Land and Sweat Equity)	$5.63
Multiplying: "Living in the fear of the Lord and encouraged by the Holy Spirit, it increased in numbers" (Acts 9:31, NIV).			
Multiplying Church Plants Over Time	4	Smaller Daughter Churches Built Within Three Years	$21.38
	5	Next-Generation Granddaughter Churches Built by Each Church	$119.81

The above table is a representative example of an ICM partner in India. Project funding, building models, and church planting replication vary by country and partner.

Appendix B

INTIMATE RELATIONSHIP
WITH GOD

—⚬⚬⚬—

T
HROUGHOUT THE SCRIPTURES we are encouraged and exhorted
to seek to know God and to please Him through carrying out
His purposes in the Earth. Here are a few examples of these life-
changing divine exhortations:

> A good man out of the good treasure of his heart brings
> forth good; and an evil man out of the evil treasure of his
> heart brings forth evil. For out of the abundance of the
> heart his mouth speaks.
> —LUKE 6:45, NKJV

> A new commandment I give to you, that you love one
> another; as I have loved you, that you also love one
> another. By this all will know that you are My disciples, if
> you have love for one another.
> —JOHN 13:34–35, NKJV

> He who would love life And see good days, Let him
> refrain his tongue from evil, And his lips from speaking
> deceit. Let him turn away from evil and do good; let him
> seek peace and pursue it.
> —1 PETER 3:10–11, NKJV

> By this my Father is glorified, that you bear much fruit; so
> you will be My disciples....You did not choose Me, but I
> chose you and appointed you that you should go and bear
> fruit, and that your fruit should remain, that whatever you
> ask the Father in My name He may give you.
> —JOHN 15:8, 16, NKJV

And whatever you do, do it heartily, as to the Lord and not to men.

—Colossians 3:23, nkjv

And this I pray, that your love may abound still more and more in knowledge and all discernment, that you may approve the things that are excellent, that you may be sincere and without offense till the day of Christ, being filled with the fruits of righteousness which are by Jesus Christ, to the glory and praise of God.

—Philippians 1:9–11, nkjv

BIBLICAL INJUNCTIONS AND PROMISES FOR GIVING

———— ⊱⊰ ————

Every man shall give as he is able, according to the blessing of the LORD thy God which he hath given thee.

—DEUTERONOMY 16:17, KJV

Then the people rejoiced, for that they offered willingly, because with perfect heart they offered willingly to the LORD: and David the king also rejoiced with great joy.

—1 CHRONICLES 29:9, KJV

Withhold not good from them to whom it is due, when it is in the power of thine hand to do it.

—PROVERBS 3:27, KJV

There is that scattereth, and yet increaseth; and there is that withholdeth more than is meet, but it tendeth to poverty. The liberal soul shall be made fat: and he that watereth shall be watered also himself.

—PROVERBS 11:24–25, KJV

[The slothful] coveteth greedily all the day long: but the righteous giveth and spareth not.

—PROVERBS 21:26, KJV

He that hath a bountiful eye shall be blessed; for he giveth of his bread to the poor.

—PROVERBS 22:9, KJV

He that giveth unto the poor shall not lack: but he that hideth his eyes shall have many a curse.

—PROVERBS 28:27, KJV

Bring ye all the tithes into the storehouse, that there may be meat in mine house, and prove me now herewith, saith the LORD of hosts, if I will not open you the windows of heaven, and pour you out a blessing, that there shall not be room enough to receive it.

—MALACHI 3:10, KJV

But when thou doest alms, let not thy left hand know what thy right hand doeth: That thine alms may be in secret: and thy Father which seeth in secret himself shall reward thee openly.

—MATTHEW 6:3–4, KJV

And Jesus sat over against the treasury, and beheld how the people cast money into the treasury: and many that were rich cast in much. And there came a certain poor widow, and she threw in two mites, which make a farthing. And he called unto him his disciples, and saith unto them, Verily I say unto you, That this poor widow hath cast more in, than all they which have cast into the treasury: For all they did cast in of their abundance; but she of her want did cast in all that she had, even all her living.

—MARK 12:41–44, KJV

He answereth and saith unto them, He that hath two coats, let him impart to him that hath none; and he that hath meat, let him do likewise.

—LUKE 3:11, KJV

Give to every man that asketh of thee; and of him that taketh away thy goods ask them not again.

—LUKE 6:30, KJV

Give, and it shall be given unto you; good measure, pressed down, and shaken together, and running over, shall men give into your bosom. For with the same measure that ye mete withal it shall be measured to you again.

—LUKE 6:38, KJV

For God so loved the world, that he gave his only begotten Son, that whosoever believeth in him should not perish, but have everlasting life.

—JOHN 3:16, KJV

I have shewed you all things, how that so labouring ye ought to support the weak, and to remember the words of the Lord Jesus, how he said, It is more blessed to give than to receive.

—ACTS 20:35, KJV

Or he that exhorteth, on exhortation: he that giveth, let him do it with simplicity; he that ruleth, with diligence; he that sheweth mercy, with cheerfulness.

—ROMANS 12:8, KJV

But this I say, He which soweth sparingly shall reap also sparingly; and he which soweth bountifully shall reap also bountifully. Every man according as he purposeth in his heart, so let him give; not grudgingly, or of necessity: for God loveth a cheerful giver. And God is able to make all grace abound toward you; that ye, always having all sufficiency in all things, may abound to every good work.

—2 CORINTHIANS 9:6–8, KJV

Now he that ministereth seed to the sower both minister bread for your food, and multiply your seed sown, and increase the fruits of your righteousness.

—2 CORINTHIANS 9:10, KJV

Now ye Philippians know also, that in the beginning of the gospel, when I departed from Macedonia, no church communicated with me as concerning giving and receiving, but ye only. For even in Thessalonica ye sent once and again unto my necessity. Not because I desire a gift: but I desire fruit that may abound to your account.

—PHILIPPIANS 4:15–17, KJV

If a brother or sister be naked, and destitute of daily food,
And one of you say unto them, Depart in peace, be ye
warmed and filled; notwithstanding ye give them not
those things which are needful to the body; what doth
it profit?

—JAMES 2:15–16, KJV

Appendix D

STATEMENT OF FAITH: INTERNATIONAL COOPERATING MINISTRIES[1]

⸺∞⸺

INTERNATIONAL COOPERATING MINISTRIES subscribes to the Lausanne Covenant, a declaration of faith agreed upon by more than 2,300 evangelical Christians during the 1974 International Congress in Lausanne, Switzerland. The Lausanne Covenant details our belief in being intentional about evangelization and the call to work together to make Jesus Christ known throughout the world.

We believe in one eternal God, Creator and Lord of the world, Father, Son, and Holy Spirit, who governs all things according to the purpose of His will.

We believe in Jesus Christ, God's Son, who is Savior and Lord, and who gave Himself as a ransom for sinners through His death on the cross. He rose from the dead and ascended to heaven, where, as truly God and truly man, Jesus is the only mediator between God and humankind.

We believe that all people are lost sinners and cannot see the Kingdom of God except through new birth. Justification is by grace through faith in Christ alone.

We believe in the power of the Holy Spirit, the very Spirit of God, sent to bear witness of the Son. We believe in the work of God's Spirit for the individual's new birth and growth, and for the Church's constant renewal in truth, wisdom, faith, holiness, love, power, and mission.

We believe the Old and New Testament Scriptures to be the only inspired, written Word of God, infallible and without error, our guide for faith and practice.

We believe in one holy, universal, and apostolic Church. The Church's calling is to worship and witness for Jesus Christ, who is the Head, preaching the Gospel among all nations and demonstrating its commitment by compassionate service to the needs of all people.

We believe that Jesus Christ will return personally and visibly in power and glory to consummate His salvation and His judgment. God will fully manifest His Kingdom when He establishes a new heaven and a new earth in which He is glorified forever and ever.

Our founder, Dois Rosser, served the Lausanne event as a board member of the conference for world evangelism. Therefore, we ascribe to the tenants of this covenant.

NOTES

INTRODUCTION

1. *Westminster Shorter Catechism*, Center for Reformed Theology and Apologetics, accessed December 2, 2014, at http://www.reformed.org/documents/WSC.html.

CHAPTER 1
THE JOY OF CATALYTIC LIVING

1. Ibid.
2. Merriam-Webster Online, s.v. "catalyst," accessed April 14, 2014, at http://www.merriam-webster.com/dictionary/catalyst.
3. Ibid., accessed November 10, 2014.
4. Augustine of Hippo, *The Confessions of Saint Augustine*, accessed June 26, 2014, at "Confessions Quotes," *Goodreads*, http://www.goodreads.com/work/quotes/1427207-confessiones on.
5. Dois Rosser, founder International Cooperating Ministries (ICM), www.icm.org/.
6. Dois I. Rosser Jr. and Ellen Vaughn, *The God Who Hung on the Cross* (Hampton Road, VA: International Cooperating Ministries, 2011), 74-75.
7. Ibid.
8. Ibid., 75.

CHAPTER 2
GRACE TRIUMPHS IN TRAGEDY

1. John Piper, *The Pleasures of God: Meditations on God's Delight in Being God* (Colorado Springs, CO: Multnomah Books, 2000).
2. Rosser and Vaughn, *The God Who Hung on the Cross*, 67–69.
3. Ibid.
4. Dick Woodward, *The Four Spiritual Secrets*, found online at "ICM's Mini Bible College with Dick Woodward," *OnePlace.com*, accessed December 2, 2014, at http://www.oneplace.com/ministries/mini-bible-college.
5. Lloyd John Ogilvie, *God's Best for My Life: A Classic Daily Devotional* (Eugene, OR: Harvest House Publishers, 2008), s.v. "June 30."

6.   John Piper, "6 Aspects of Humility," *Desiring God*, March 13, 2008, accessed December 2, 2014, at http://www.desiringgod.org/blog/posts/6-aspects-of-humility.

7.   Jessica Burchfield, "Building the Kingdom One Day at a Time," *TwoTen Magazine* 8(2014): accessed December 2, 2014, at http://www.twotenmag.com/icm. See more at http://www.twotenmag.com/icm#sthash.oRoRLWdl.dpuf.

8.   "The Templeton Prize is awarded annually" by a "panel of distinguished judges" to recognize an individual who brings "new understandings in the quest for progress in humanity's efforts to comprehend the many and diverse manifestations of the Divine." Found at "Nomination Procedure," *Templeton Prize*, accessed December 2, 2014, at http://templetonprize.org/nomination.html.

9.   Please visit our Web site at www.stlukeseye.com.

10.   Rosser and Vaughn, *The God Who Hung on the Cross*, 82.

11.   Passages referenced include 1 Corinthians 3:9, Ephesians 2:20–22, and 1 Peter 2:4-5. To access this insightful article, please go to Brian Smith, "A Consultative Report for ICM," at www.icm.org.

12.   Augustine, quoted in Ibid.

Chapter 3
Catalytic Entrepreneurs

1.   Rick Warren, *The Purpose Driven Life* (Grand Rapids, MI: Zondervan, 2002), 281.

Chapter 4
Joy-Filled Accounts of Catalytic Givers

1.   Mother Teresa, quoted at *BrainyQuote*, accessed August 7, 2013, at http://www.brainyquote.com/.

2.   Mother Teresa, quoted at *ThinkExist*, accessed August 7, 2013, at http://thinkexist.com/quotes/mother_teresa_of_calcutta/.

3.   Merriam-Webster Online, s.v. "catalyst," accessed April 14, 2014.

Chapter 5
Elevated to Servanthood

1.   Charles D. Meigs, "Lord, Help Me Live from Day to Day," accessed December 2, 2014, at http://www.hymnary.org/text/lord_help_me_live_from_day_in_such_a_sel.

2.   D L Moody, *Secret Power*, Chapter 2, accessed December 2, 2014, at www.inthebeginning.com/articles/moody2.htm.

3.   Jonathan Aitken, "Remembering Charles Colson, A Man Transformed," *Christianity Today*, April 21, 2012, accessed January

22, 2014, at http://www.christianitytoday.com/ct/2012/aprilweb-only/charles-colson-aitken.html?start=3.

4. Ibid.

5. Ibid.

6. Ibid.

7. *Westminster Shorter Catechism*, Center for Reformed Theology and Apologetics.

8. John Piper, "6 Aspects of Humility," *Desiring God.*

CHAPTER 6
INSPIRED BY GENEROUS GIVERS, INC.

1. John Piper, quoted at "John Piper Quotes," *Goodreads,* accessed December 2, 2014, at http://www.goodreads.com/author/quotes/25423.John_Piper.

2. "Sheila Johnson," Bio, A&E Television Networks, accessed November 30, 2013, at http://www.biography.com/people/sheila-johnson-17112944.

3. Kam Williams, "Interview with America's First Black Billionairess, Sheila C. Johnson," *BlackNews.com,* accessed December 2, 2014, at http://blacknews.com/news/sheila_johnson_interview101.shtml#.Upo3YGSidLc.

4. "Our Beliefs," *Generous Giving,* accessed January 26, 2013, at http://www.generousgiving.org/beliefs.

CHAPTER 7
FULFILLING YOUR DESTINY

1. Mother Teresa, quoted at *BrainyQuote,* accessed August 7, 2013, at http://www.brainyquote.com/.

2. Please visit our Web site at www.stlukeseye.com.

3. Mother Teresa, quoted at *BrainyQuote.*

4. Ibid.

EPILOGUE:
TRIBUTE TO AN EXCEPTIONAL SERVANT OF GOD

1. A video of Dick Woodward's memorial service may be found at "Dick Woodard's Memorial Service—Saturday, March 15, 2014," vimeo.com/89240946.

2. "Dick Woodward," *International Cooperating Ministries,* accessed March 20, 2014, at www.icm.org/dickwoodward.

Appendix D
Statement of Faith: International Cooperating Ministries (ICM)

1.   International Cooperating Ministries' Statement of Faith may be found at http://www.icm.org/about-us/statement-of-faith.

ABOUT THE AUTHOR

⸺⸱⸺

D R. JAMES P. Gills received his medical degree from Duke University Medical Center in 1959 and served his ophthalmology residency at the Wilmer Ophthalmological Institute of Johns Hopkins University from 1962–1965. He founded St. Luke's Cataract and Laser Institute in Tarpon Springs, Florida, and has performed more cataract and lens implant surgeries than any other eye surgeon in the world. Since establishing his Florida practice in 1968, he has been firmly committed to embracing new technology and perfecting the latest cataract surgery techniques. In 1974, he became the first eye surgeon in the US to dedicate his practice to cataract treatment through the use of intraocular lenses. Dr. Gills has been recognized in Florida and throughout the world for his professional accomplishments and personal commitment to helping others. He has been recognized by the readers of *Cataract & Refractive Surgery Today* as one of the top fifty cataract and refractive opinion leaders.

Dr. Gills is not only known for his skills as a doctor but his skill in business as president of a variety of companies, including as past president of the World Triathlon Corporation (Ironman). He received the 1990 Entrepreneur of the Year Award from the State of Florida, the 2000 Florida Enterprise Medal by the Merchant's Association of Florida, Inc., the 2000 Free Enterpriser of the Year Award from the Florida Council on Economic Education, the Tampa Bay Ethics Award, and an appointment to the Florida Sports Foundation Board of Directors. He is an avid athlete and has competed in 46 marathons, 30 triathlons, 5 Ironman races, 6 double Irons, and 4 two-hundred-mile races. He has published over 195 medical articles and authored or co-authored 10 books on ophthalmology. He has also written 20 books on Christian living, with over 6 million in print. Dr. Gills' philanthropic work in over 70 ministries and organizations led to him being awarded the Duke University 2005 Humanitarian Award and the 2002 William Carey Award for Extraordinary Leadership and Service in World Missions, presented by Trinity College.

Married in 1962, Dr. Gills and his wife, Heather, have raised two children, Shea and Pit. Shea Gills Grundy, a former attorney and now full-time mom, is a graduate of Vanderbilt University and Emory Law School. She and husband Shane Grundy, MD, have four children: twins, Maggie and Braddock; Jimmy; and Lily Grace. The Gills' son, J. Pit Gills, MD, ophthalmologist, received his medical degree from Duke University Medical Center and in 2001 joined the practice at St. Luke's. "Dr. Pit" is married to Joy Gills. They have three children: Pitzer, Parker, and Stokes.